MACMILLAN MAS

GENERAL EDITOR: JAMES GIBSON

Published

JANE AUSTEN	*Emma* Norman Page
	Sense and Sensibility Judy Simons
	Pride and Prejudice Raymond Wilson
	Mansfield Park Richard Wirdnam
SAMUEL BECKETT	*Waiting for Godot* Jennifer Birkett
WILLIAM BLAKE	*Songs of Innocence* and *Songs of Experience* Alan Tomlinson
ROBERT BOLT	*A Man for all Seasons* Leonard Smith
EMILY BRONTË	*Wuthering Heights* Hilda D. Spear
GEOFFREY CHAUCER	*The Miller's Tale* Michael Alexander
	The Pardoner's Tale Geoffrey Lester
	The Prologue to the Canterbury Tales Nigel Thomas and Richard Swan
CHARLES DICKENS	*Bleak House* Dennis Butts
	Great Expectations Dennis Butts
	Hard Times Norman Page
GEORGE ELIOT	*Middlemarch* Graham Handley
	Silas Marner Graham Handley
	The Mill on the Floss Helen Wheeler
HENRY FIELDING	*Joseph Andrews* Trevor Johnson
E. M. FORSTER	*Howards End* Ian Milligan
	A Passage to India Hilda D. Spear
WILLIAM GOLDING	*The Spire* Rosemary Sumner
	Lord of the Flies Raymond Wilson
OLIVER GOLDSMITH	*She Stoops to Conquer* Paul Ranger
THOMAS HARDY	*The Mayor of Casterbridge* Ray Evans
	Tess of the D'Urbervilles James Gibson
	Far from the Madding Crowd Colin Temblett-Wood
JOHN KEATS	*Selected Poems* John Garrett
PHILIP LARKIN	*The Whitsun Weddings* and *The Less Deceived* Andrew Swarbrick
D. H. LAWRENCE	*Sons and Lovers* R. P. Draper
HARPER LEE	*To Kill a Mockingbird* Jean Armstrong
CHRISTOPHER MARLOWE	*Doctor Faustus* David A. Male
THE METAPHYSICAL POETS	Joan van Emden

MACMILLAN MASTER GUIDES

THOMAS MIDDLETON and WILLIAM ROWLEY	*The Changeling*	Tony Bromham
ARTHUR MILLER	*The Crucible*	Leonard Smith
GEORGE ORWELL	*Animal Farm*	Jean Armstrong
WILLIAM SHAKESPEARE	*Richard II*	Charles Barber
	Hamlet	Jean Brooks
	King Lear	Francis Casey
	Henry V	Peter Davison
	The Winter's Tale	Diana Devlin
	Julius Caesar	David Elloway
	Macbeth	David Elloway
	Measure for Measure	Mark Lilly
	Henry IV Part I	Helen Morris
	Romeo and Juliet	Helen Morris
	The Tempest	Kenneth Pickering
	A Midsummer Night's Dream	Kenneth Pickering
GEORGE BERNARD SHAW	*St Joan*	Leonée Ormond
RICHARD SHERIDAN	*The School for Scandal*	Paul Ranger
	The Rivals	Jeremy Rowe
ALFRED TENNYSON	*In Memoriam*	Richard Gill
JOHN WEBSTER	*The White Devil* and *The Duchess of Malfi*	David A. Male

Forthcoming

CHARLOTTE BRONTË	*Jane Eyre*	Robert Miles
JOHN BUNYAN	*The Pilgrim's Progress*	Beatrice Batson
JOSEPH CONRAD	*The Secret Agent*	Andrew Mayne
T. S. ELIOT	*Murder in the Cathedral*	Paul Lapworth
	Selected Poems	Andrew Swarbrick
GERARD MANLEY HOPKINS	*Selected Poems*	R. Watt
BEN JONSON	*Volpone*	Michael Stout
RUDYARD KIPLING	*Kim*	Leonée Ormond
ARTHUR MILLER	*Death of a Salesman*	Peter Spalding
JOHN MILTON	*Comus*	Tom Healy
WILLIAM SHAKESPEARE	*Othello*	Tony Bromham
	As You Like It	Kiernan Ryan
	Coriolanus	Gordon Williams
	Antony and Cleopatra	Martin Wine
ANTHONY TROLLOPE	*Barchester Towers*	Ken Newton
VIRGINIA WOOLF	*To the Lighthouse*	John Mepham
	Mrs Dalloway	Julian Pattison
W. B. YEATS	*Selected Poems*	Stan Smith

MACMILLAN MASTER GUIDES
SELECTED POEMS OF
JOHN KEATS

JOHN GARRETT

MACMILLAN
EDUCATION

First edition 1987

Published by
MACMILLAN EDUCATION LTD
Houndmills, Basingstoke, Hampshire RG21 2XS
and London
Companies and representatives
throughout the world

Typeset by
TEC SET, Sutton, Surrey

Printed in Hong Kong

British Library Cataloguing in Publication Data
Garrett, John
Selected poems of John Keats.—
(Macmillan master guides)
1. Keats, John, 1795–1821—Study and
teaching—Outlines, syllabi, etc.
I. Title
821′.7   PR4832
ISBN 0–333–42286–4 Pbk
ISBN 0–333–42287–2 Pbk export

CONTENTS

GENERAL EDITOR'S PREFACE

The aim of the Macmillan Master Guides is to help you to appreciate the book you are studying by providing information about it and by suggesting ways of reading and thinking about it which will lead to a fuller understanding. The section on the writer's life and background has been designed to illustrate those aspects of the writer's life which have influenced the work, and to place it in its personal and literary context. The summaries and critical commentary are of special importance in that each brief summary of the action is followed by an examination of the significant critical points. The space which might have been given to repetitive explanatory notes has been devoted to a detailed analysis of the kind of passage which might confront you in an examination. Literary criticism is concerned with both the broader aspects of the work being studied and with its detail. The ideas which meet us in reading a great work of literature, and their relevance to us today, are an essential part of our study, and our Guides look at the thought of their subject in some detail. But just as essential is the craft with which the writer has constructed his work of art, and this may be considered under several technical headings — characterisation, language, style and stagecraft, for example.

The authors of these Guides are all teachers and writers of wide experience, and they have chosen to write about books they admire and know well in the belief that they can communicate their admiration to you. But you yourself must read and know intimately the book you are studying. No one can do that for you. You should see this book as a lamp-post. Use it to shed light, not to lean against. If you know your text and know what it is saying about life, and how it says it, then you will enjoy it, and there is no better way of passing an examination in literature.

JAMES GIBSON

ACKNOWLEDGEMENT

Cover illustration: *The Enchanted Castle* by Claude. Reproduced by Courtesy of the Trustees, The National Gallery, London.

This book is dedicated to Jassem Lawrence

1 JOHN KEATS:
LIFE AND BACKGROUND

1.1 KEATS'S LIFE

John Keats's origins were lowly, though not as abject as was made out later in his life by critics trying to consign him to the 'Cockney school of poetry'. His father was head ostler at a London inn, a promotion he probably gained on marrying Keat's mother, whose father held the lease of the inn. John, born on 31 October 1795, was the first of five children (one died in infancy), and developed strong relationships with his brothers George and Tom and, to a lesser extent, with his young sister Fanny. His parents were affluent enough to send himself and George to the private school of John Clarke in Enfield, a more enlightened institution than its counterparts, Dotheboys Hall or Mr Creakle's Establishment, in Charles Dickens's novels. Here Keats benefited not only from the liberal atmosphere which encouraged independence of character, but from his friendship with the headmaster's son, Charles Cowden Clarke, eight years his senior, who guided his taste in reading and provided him with the all-important introduction to the literary circle of James Henry Leigh Hunt.

Keats was able to continue at Clarke's school, despite losing his father at the age of eight and his mother six years later. These early years were plagued by sudden accident and emotional turmoil. His mother took a second husband only two months after Keats's father had been fatally thrown from his horse: a precipitate remarriage that may have been behind Keats's later identification of himself with Shakespeare's Hamlet. After a dispute over a family will, Mrs Keats (now Mrs Rawlings) deserted her children, who were reared by their maternal grandmother for a number of years. His mother finally made her peace and reappeared in Keats's life, only to be snatched away a year later by tuberculosis, the family disease. Domestic instability may account for Keats's mercurial temperament. Though small of stature, he had as a schoolboy a reputation for belligerence, even attacking a master for some perceived injustice to his brother George. His volatile personality found release later in violent switches of mood from luxurious ecstasy to profound depression (as an adolescent he threatened to kill himself if he could not become a poet), and also in one of the most essential characteristics of his poetry: a continual vacillation between the attractiveness of an escape-world, a paradise created by literature or art, and the intrusive insistence of the real world of pain, sorrow and human insufficiency.

'Money troubles' were to pester Keats for the rest of his life, often interrupting his compositions in mid-career. The litigation that split his family when he was a child gave him a morbid loathing of pecuniary transactions, so much so that in later life to 'stand in the bank an hour or two' seemed to him a torture 'worse than anything in Dante'. Financial uncertainty was no doubt partly responsible for Keats's decision to leave school at 15 and begin a five-year apprenticeship as an apothecary, a course of action approved by his level-headed guardian, Richard Abbey. During this time Keats continued to study literature in a rather dilettante manner under the tutelage of Charles Cowden Clarke and, although he wrote some verses at the age of 18 in imitation of Edmund Spenser (along with a few other inconsequential poems), he showed little sign at this time of possessing any unique gift. Poetically he was a late developer.

In 1815, his apprenticeship completed, Keats entered Guys Hospital as a trainee surgeon. Throughout the following year his absorption by poetry grew stronger, conflicting more and more with his medical studies and engendering in him the fear that the blood-and-bone reality of his chosen métier might kill in him the ability to see life poetically, might banish 'elf and fay' from the purlieus of his imagination.

> I am oft in doubt whether at all
> I shall again see Phoebus in the morning,

he wrote in a verse-letter ('To George Felton Mathew') during this period: the sordid sights and smells of the dissecting room threatened to remove the mystic veil from life, to reduce the personified sun-god Phoebus to a mere ball of hot gas. Keats's decision to abandon the medical profession and devote himself entirely to poetry was taken on the eve of his twenty-first birthday, and it horrified his guardian (Abbey later recalled having castigated Keats as 'a silly boy and prophesied a speedy termination to his inconsiderate enterprise'). It was a brave and momentous decision on Keats's part for, although the meeting with Hunt had by now taken place and his first significant poem, the 'Chapman's Homer' sonnet, had achieved some recognition, the world of poetry lay all before him and his talent for advancement in it was largely untested. It is small wonder that he sometimes saw himself at this stage in terms of 'a sick Eagle looking at the sky'.

He persevered in his choice, nevertheless, and the next four years witnessed a rapid development in Keats's understanding of literature, of life, and of how he stood in relation to both. It was a continuing process of self-education, and each poem that was struck off in the course of it exhibits a fresh standpoint and testifies to Keats's accelerated progress towards precocious maturity as both poet and philosopher. Keats took the materials of his life and forged poetry out of them, so that nothing that happened to him was wasted. Even his medical training had its part to play, lending a hard concreteness to much of his imagery, and producing phrases such as 'the wreath'd trellis of a working brain' (in 'Ode to Psyche') which combine objective anatomical fact with the fertile creations of 'the gardener Fancy'.

In order to equip himself as a poet, Keats plunged into the study of poetry with 'gusto' (a favourite expression of his). He read avidly in the works of earlier, and some contemporary poets, all the time living on what was left to him, after the expenses of his medical training, of a small legacy from his mother's branch of the family. This was a period of passive receptivity, sometimes referred to by Keats self-deprecatingly as 'indolence', interspersed with bouts of active creation that produced rather immature works ('mawkish' or 'weak-sided', in Keats's remorseless words of self-criticism) such as *Endymion* and 'Isabella'. Keats was preparing himself for the great task that lay ahead, which, he thought, must be the production, like his great precursors Spenser and Milton, of a long heroic poem, since 'epic was of all the king'. The preparation involved not only an intensive reading course, but the experience of different scenes from which the materials of future poetry could be gathered. To this end Keats journeyed restlessly around the south of England. Then in the summer of 1818, just after his brother George had married and emigrated to America, Keats embarked on his most ambitious excursion, a 1000-mile tour, largely on foot, of the Lake District and Scotland (a brief visit to Northern Ireland was also slotted in) with his friend Charles Brown. This expedition was explicitly undertaken to imbibe grandiose scenery for Keat's next poem ('I shall learn poetry here', he affirmed), and the Scottish Highlands, transported to the Aegean Sea, duly appeared as the background to 'Hyperion':

> Crag jutting forth to crag, and rocks that seemed
> Ever as if just rising from a sleep. (II, 10–11)

After a long wet trudge across the Isle of Mull, Keats fell ill with a severe cold, and returned to London to find that his brother Tom was in the last stages of a tubercular infection.

If the walking tour gave sublimity to Keats's conception of the natural world, Tom's fatal illness added depth to his perception of its sorrows. For the last three months of 1818 he nursed Tom on his death-bed, seeking relief by beginning work on 'Hyperion'. The disintegration of one was compensated to some extent by his attempt to shape the elements of the other. After Tom's death Keats 'leaped headlong' into poetic creation, producing over the next nine months the five major odes and his most accomplished narratives. He also encountered the next, and last, formative influence on his life: Fanny Brawne.

The 18-year-old Fanny and her mother became Keats's neighbours, taking the other half of the house that Keats was sharing with Charles Brown in Wentworth Place, Hampstead. Despite showing no great interest in poetry, she exerted, from the start of their acquaintance, a strong fascination upon Keats, who found her unconventionally forthright manner – 'calling people such names that I was forced . . . to make use of the term *Minx*' – refreshing after the simpering coyness of other lady friends, such as the sisters of fellow-poet John Reynolds. The relationship quickly intensified from playfulness to a more serious attachment, and it is possible that aspects of Fanny's character, or of Keats's reading of it, found their way positively into 'The Eve of St Agnes' and negatively into 'Lamia' and 'La Belle Dame sans Merci'. Keats, fearful lest his love for Fanny divert him from the goal he had set himself of being 'among the English poets after my death', left London for three months in the summer of 1819, to devote himself to the demands of his other mistress, his 'demon Poesy', writing 'Lamia', the play *Otho the Great* and the last of the great odes, 'To Autumn', in the Isle of Wight and Winchester. The strain of being absent from Fanny made the calling of poetry seem even lonelier than before: 'at night, when the lonely day has closed . . . the lonely, silent, unmusical chamber is waiting to receive me as into a sepulchre', he wrote to her from Shanklin. His pursuit of poetry was leading him into uncharted territory, and his refusal to use it any longer as a vehicle for escape was forcing him to face some disquieting configurations of the nature of reality. 'Deathwards progressing/ To no death' is the visage of his poetic mentor Moneta in the unfinished 'Fall of Hyperion'.

Reports of financial disaster from George in America curtailed Keats's creative activity in the autumn of 1819. Drained by the strenuous efforts of the year's writing just completed, and torn between his desire for Fanny and his realisation that to succumb to it might mean the sacrifice of his poetical self, Keats was ill prepared for the severe haemorrhage that struck him on 3 February 1820. His medical knowledge told him at once what it meant: 'I cannot be deceived in that colour. That drop of blood is my death warrant', he said to Brown. The family disease had struck him down. Henceforth

Keats's life became increasingly hopeless in all its prospects, a 'posthumous existence' as he called it. In health he had been able to accept stoically the public's indifference to his first collection of poems (published in 1817) and the critical derision unleashed by *Endymion* (1818). Now, when his third book was at last gaining recognition for its author, Keats was past caring. His affair with Fanny Brawne was as torturous as ever. Unofficially engaged, to the hostile disapproval of both his friends and her family, and with his financial resources apparently exhausted, Keats knew that Fanny was further beyond his reach than ever. 'I eternally see her figure eternally vanishing', he wrote to Charles Brown.

His friends rallied round to send him to Italy and one of them, the painter Joseph Severn, accompanied him on a tempestuous sea voyage, ending in a steamy quarantine in Naples that cannot have been therapeutic. Ironically, Keats finally beheld the country that he had wished to visit as part of his plan to 'get wisdom – get understanding' through a veil of sickness, in the last desperate attempt to stave off death. Italy, instead of being the hoped-for academy of the soul, was reduced to the role of the body's sanatorium. After a four-month decline Keats died in Rome on 23 February 1821, at the age of 25. Despite the destruction of all his earthly hopes, his lack of conviction in any life after death, and his belief that even the fame he had fought so hard to attain as a poet had finally eluded him – 'Here lies one whose name was writ in water' was the epitaph he requested for his grave – Keats did not go down wallowing in self-pity. His sense of humour he retained when everything else was lost. Remarking on the anticlimax towards which his life was headed, he wrote to Fanny Brawne in March 1820: 'there is a great difference between going off in warm blood like Romeo, and making one's exit like a frog in a frost'. His last written words, to Brown, were similarly self-effacing: 'I can scarcely bid you goodbye even in a letter. I always made an awkward bow'. The poems he left behind, compressed out of a short, harrowing, but intensely lived, adulthood, are arguably the richest legacy of the Romantic era.

1.2 ROMANTICISM

The pressure against the 'classical' Augustan writers – those such as Alexander Pope and Samuel Johnson who set the style in poetry and prose for a carefully weighed consideration of the universe set down in judiciously chosen language – was increasing gradually throughout the eighteenth century, vapourising occasionally in the odd work indicative of the eruption to come. Thomas Gray's 'Elegy Written in a Country Churchyard' (1751), for example, shows the poet half-turning his back on the urban civilisation so central to the Augustan construct of a rationally ordered existence, and looking instead towards the comforts offered by rural nature; while in prose Horace Walpole's *Castle of Otranto* (1764) took the lid off the unconscious, and permitted ghosts to mingle with the human personae that had normally been the sole occupants of fictional works. Such manifestations of dissatisfaction with an inordinately logical view of life were, however, exceptional until the last decade of the century.

Literary revolt in England coincided with political upheaval in France. The work that heralded the Romantic movement, William Blake's *Songs of Innocence*, appeared in the same year as the French Revolution, 1789. Both were events that signalled the end of the status quo. For the next 40 years Europe was in the throes of a turbulent transformation, cultural, political and economic (the Industrial Revolution was gathering steam at this time). It was in the process of acquiring a new character, of becoming something else: the theme of fluid identity is often located in the protagonist of Romantic poetry.

By the late 1820s the release of pent-up emotional and intellectual energy that found expression in Romantic verse had largely spent itself. But Romantic ideas continued to exert an influence for the remainder of the century. Romanticism added a dye to the stream of English literature which still leaves traces in the late twentieth century. Some of the main features of Romanticism (they were not all new elements, but rather new emphases) may be listed.

Nature
No longer to be feared or regarded as a nuisance, the natural world took on special significance for the Romantics, either as a sign of the 'Presence' of the invisible Creator in the works of William Wordsworth, or as a sublime backdrop to the stupendous psychodrama of the Romantic hero. Lord Byron's *Childe Harold*, for instance, becomes one with the elements that rage around him:

> I am as a weed
> Flung from the rock, on Ocean's foam to sail
> Where'er the surge may sweep, the tempest's breath prevail;

while in fiction Mary Shelley's Dr Frankenstein sees the monster he has created approaching him in the Alpine mountains across a 'vast river of ice' which exteriorises the glacier that his heart, numbed by forbidden studies, has become.

Nature in its gentler moods was also congenial to the Romantics, as Wordsworth's encomium on the 'host' of daffodils at Ullswater makes clear. In either its sublime or its merely beautiful aspect, nature was preferred in its untamed state. The Augustans, on the other hand, liked nature to be cultivated, and looked with a kindly eye on manifestations of man's interference, as Pope ilustrates in 'Windsor Forest', where 'midst the desert fruitful fields arise'.

Individual psychology
The psychology of the individual was explored by the Romantics as never before. The interior landscape – the mind of the protagonist – became a terrain as replete with adventure and discovery as had been the objective locations of the eighteenth-century novel. The unconscious was given special attention, and dreams provided the starting point for many an evocative or provocative poem (S.T. Coleridge's 'Kubla Khan', for instance). The unconscious might offer a clue to the mystery of existence and, because it finds relatively freer expression in children and uneducated people, infants and peasants are often focused upon by the Romantic poet.

Rejection of orthodox religion
Religion is seen as an institution built by the human mind at a time obsessed by the need to define everything, even God. The Christian church is one of the 'mind-forged manacles' that Blake complains of: it imprisons rather than liberates, and kills the human spirit instead of fostering it. In the place of conventional religion the Romantics substituted the individual quest for personal enlightenment. The discovery of God becomes a private affair, arrived at after a strenuous and darkling voyage. The metaphor of the journey is dominant in Romantic poetry, from Percy Bysshe Shelley's several subterranean boat trips to the caverns of the unconscious, to Blake's ranging across the cosmos in his prophetic books, and to Wordsworth's lengthy autobiographical travels in *The Prelude* which constitute a simultaneous exploration of experience, of 'emotion recollected in tranquility', and of the lessons it has to teach. The apprehension of God, and the confidence in His existence, varies widely from one Romantic to another.

Revolutionary politics
The Romantics were generally sympathetic to the cause of revolution in politics, particularly during their youth:

> Bliss was it in that dawn to be alive,
> But to be young was very heaven,

said Wordsworth, recalling his first reaction to the French Revolution. Since the institutions of government were also the product of the human mind rather than the human soul – 'classical' rather than 'Romantic' in spirit – they were as obsolescent as conventional religion. The Romantics wanted not only a regeneration, through revolution, of society, but also a renewal, through psychological catharsis, of the individual man or woman. The emphasis shifted from poet to poet, with Wordsworth concentrating on individual 'growth' in *The Prelude* and Shelley more anarchistically hoping for a revolution 'among mankind' in 'Ode to the West Wind'.

Simplicity of diction

Wordsworth, in his 1802 Preface to *Lyrical Ballads*, rejected the somewhat artificial 'poetic diction' favoured by his eighteenth-century predecessors, and vowed instead to deploy in his verse only the 'language really used by men'. Instead of adopting the sort of language that people had grown to expect from a poem, language suitable for eliciting stock responses in the course of an argument proceeding in pedestrian fashion on iambic feet within rhyming couplets, the Romantics sought to refresh the language of poetry, to employ it as the vehicle for the unexpected and the suggestively symbolic, and to make it correspond as exactly as possible to the emotion that it evoked. Diction takes on a new subjective sincerity that is complementary to the mood of confessional honesty that prevails in Romantic verse. As an example, here is Coleridge musing on the isolation of adulthood in 'Frost at Midnight':

> And so I brooded all the following morn,
> . . . mine eye
> Fixed with mock study on my swimming book:
> Save if the door half opened, and I snatched
> A hasty glance, and still my heart leaped up,
> For still I hoped to see the stranger's face,
> Townsman, or aunt, or sister more beloved,
> My play-mate when we both were clothed alike!

Every word is appropriate to the situation. The despondency of the narrator is authentically transferred to a senseless object, so that it is the book rather than his listless mind that appears to be 'swimming'. The diction is commonplace ('Townsman, or aunt, or sister'), even banal ('My play-mate'): only in the context of the poet's painful self-disclosure, and with the aid of the cadence afforded it by the metre, does it become redolent of a deeper, more universal significance.

1.3 KEATS'S PLACE IN THE ROMANTIC MOVEMENT

Keats was the youngest of the six major Romantic poets and belongs to what is sometimes called the 'second generation' of the movement, Blake, Wordsworth and Coleridge having blazed the trail two decades before. The other younger Romantics were Byron and

Shelley. True to the individualism that Romanticism tended to encourage, each of these poets worked largely independently of the others, though their paths crossed from time to time. Wordsworth and Coleridge had collaborated on the 1798 collection of *Lyrical Ballads*, though they afterwards went separate ways.

Shelley and Keats were both championed by Leigh Hunt, who published their early poems in his weekly *Examiner* while both were still unknown. Introduced to each other by Hunt at his cottage in the Vale of Health, Hampstead, Shelley and Keats maintained a distant but respectful, professional rather than personal, friendship with each other until Keats's death, which Shelley commemorated in his poem 'Adonais'. He had generously offered to accommodate Keats at his villa in Pisa during Keats's final illness, but there was always a hint of condescension in his attitude to his junior, lower-class colleague. 'In poetry *I* have sought to avoid system and mannerism', he wrote to Keats in criticism of *Endymion*; to which Keats responded with some astute observations on Shelley's own literary tics: 'You I am sure will forgive me for sincerely remarking that you might curb your magnanimity and be more of an artist, and "load every rift" of your subject with ore'. Despite such sparring, the two poets recognised each other's worth, and when Shelley was drowned a year after Keats's death a copy of the latter's 1820 poems was found in his pocket.

The more classical temper and satirical streak of Byron rendered him less congenial to Keats, and there are scattered derogatory references to Byron and his works, whose 'themes/Are ugly cubs ('Sleep and Poetry'), throughout Keats's writings. Byron returned the favour by stigmatising Keats's poems as the product of 'mental masturbation' and their creator as a 'miserable self-polluter of the human mind'.

Of the three first-generation Romantics, Keats seems to have been ignorant of the existence of the pioneer, Blake. He did, however, make the acquaintance, through Leigh Hunt, of Wordsworth and Coleridge. He was already familiar with Wordsworth through his published work, and was one of the first to appreciate the philosophical calibre of Wordsworth's verse and not just its more popular lyrical quality. One of Keats's early poems, 'I stood tip-toe upon a little hill', is an undeclared tribute to Wordsworth with its linkage of the impressions made by nature on the speaker to the expansion of his mental or spiritual self. Keats later criticised the 'egotist' strain of Wordsworth's poetry, its self-centred absorption with its creator's intellectual evolution, and he contrasted Wordsworth's 'egotistical sublime' (the arrival at an illuminating general truth through a meticulous examination of personal emotions and the effect of experience on them) with his own self-effacing stance of 'negative capability' (the ability to leave the private self in abeyance and allow the imagination to drift free of all personal and moral moorings). But he cherished a high regard for Wordsworth's mental energy and integrity, his commitment to following a stream of thought to its source, and this aspect of Wordsworth, revealed in 'Tintern Abbey', influenced Keats's own perception of life as a 'mansion of many apartments'.

Coleridge's influence on Keats was less profound (though in a casual conversation on Hampstead Heath he may have suggested the central symbol of 'Ode to a Nightingale'). Keats was chiefly indebted to him for his notion of the 'shaping spirit of Imagination' (in the 'Dejection' ode), which gave Keats the confidence to claim that the imagination could create its own truth, 'whether it existed before or not'.

His fellow Romantics were not the only influences that operated on Keats. Spenser was an early model, and Keats became steeped in Shakespeare, whom he regarded as the 'good genius presiding over' him. Despite enormous differences in temperament and aim, he admired John Milton and eventually abandoned 'Hyperion', he said, because 'there were too many Miltonic inversions in it'. There are echoes in his work of 'pre-Romantic' poets: for example, the 'musk-rose blowing . . . far from all men's knowing' (in 'Sleep and Poetry') recalls the rose that is 'born to blush unseen' in Gray's 'Elegy', while the late ode 'To Autumn' inherits some of its imagery and much of its spirit from Thomas Chatterton ('I always somehow associate Chatterton with autumn', he remarked).

Keats ranged widely, not only in his sources, but in what he made of them: he was anything but exclusively 'Romantic'. Well aware of the lush effusiveness of his early verse, he took pains after *Endymion* to weed it out, even before the critics took him to task for it. Keats's tendency to Romantic excess – the enthusiasm of the dreamer – was always ballasted by a clear consciousness of physical reality, perhaps a heritage from his medical days. Having enjoyed the 'ethereal' spectacle of a waterfall in the Lake District, Keats turned his attention to other needs and tucked into a 'monstrous breakfast' at his hotel. The conviction that grew upon him that poetry must include all of life's experiences, even 'the miseries of the world', renders him in the last analysis one of the least romantic of Romantic poets.

1.4 THE PUBLICATION OF KEATS'S POEMS

Keats published three volumes in his lifetime. The first was brought out by Charles and James Ollier in 1817, and was called simply *Poems*. It gathered together much of Keats's juvenilia, not all of which merited preservation in print. Among the more substantial pieces were the 'Chapman's Homer' and 'Great spirits' sonnets, the verse-letters to George Felton Mathew, Charles Cowden Clarke and

George Keats, and the reflective poems 'I stood tip-toe' and 'Sleep and Poetry'. The book was largely ignored, though reviewed kindly by Keats's friends. Left with an unexpectedly large number of copies on their hands, the Olliers wrote to George Keats, 'We regret that your brother ever requested us to publish his book'. A copy given to Wordsworth by Keats was found after the former's death 33 years later with its pages still uncut.

Keats's next book, *Endymion: A Poetic Romance*, was published a year later by Taylor and Hessey. John Taylor was more sympathetic to Keats than the Olliers had been and, having confidence that 'for poetic genius there is not his equal living', advanced Keats money on the strength of it, even after all hope of a profit on *Endymion* had been shot down by the critics. Taylor's reader was Richard Wood-house, who quickly understood Keats's qualities as both man and poet. Woodhouse became a valuable friend and performed the role of literary midwife to some of Keats's narrative poems.

In 1820 Taylor and Hessey published Keats's last volume, *Lamia, The Eve of St Agnes, and Other Poems*. This time critical approval was more forthcoming, though Keats lamented that 'the sale of my book is very slow'. The book contained the work of Keats's 'annus mirabilis' (autumn 1818 – autumn 1819), with the exception of 'La Belle Dame sans Merci', and established Keats as a major voice, although he himself, mortally ill by now, wrote disparagingly of it to Shelley: 'Most of the poems . . . would never have been published but from a hope of gain'.

The first collected edition of Keats's poems was produced by Galignani of Paris in 1829. In England John Taylor, discouraged by the sluggish sales of the 1820 volume, abandoned his intention of compiling a complete edition of Keats, declaring that 'the world cares nothing for him'. Eventually, however, the demand for Keats's work increased, and the first comprehensive collection appeared in 1848, under the editorship of Richard Monckton Milnes.

1.5 KEATS'S LETTERS

Keats produced a steady stream of letters: to his brothers, his sister, his friends and fellow poets, his publishers and, finally, his fiancée. The letters are as rich in tonal range and as provocative in thought as his poems, and deserve to be studied for the light they shed on the latter at the same time as they constitute a developing drama in their own right, the drama of Keats's short but brilliant, meteor-like existence. They offer an absorbing and educative reading experience, demonstrating the truth of Keats's claim in one of them that 'A man's life of any worth is a continual allegory'.

There is a constant cross-fertilisation between letters and poems. Particular references in one context reoccur in another, with corresponding shifts in meaning. For instance, the 'Savour of poisonous brass and metal sick' that sours the palate of the sun-god Hyperion suggests the aftertaste of the mercury with which Keats intermittently dosed himself, an image which reappears as a metaphor for psychological bitterness in his last letter to Fanny Brawne: 'The last two years taste like brass upon my palate'. Objects recorded passively from his travels and experiences become transmuted into dynamic symbols in subsequent poems. The 'thickly wooded' country noted on a coach journey to Southampton is transformed into a symbol of Saturn's spiritual concussion in 'Hyperion' ('Forest on forest hung above his head').

Keats's letters vibrate with emotion and sparkle with intellect. They shimmer with compassion and wade through depression. A sense of Keats's humanity soon emerges from them. 'Men should bear with each other – there lives not the man who may not be cut up, aye hashed to pieces on his weakest side', he wrote to his friend Benjamin Bailey in 1818. As well as recording Keats's awareness of the vulnerability of human beings, the letters reveal his growing confidence in his own exceptional talent, counterpoised by a consistent sense of humour. In an early letter to Benjamin Haydon, in which he asserts that his work as a poet is superior to that of the Creator – 'looking upon the sun, the moon, the stars, the earth and its contents as materials to form greater things – that is to say ethereal things' – he breaks off to remark, with timely humility, 'but here I am talking like a madman'. After advancing some pioneering poetic theories to Reynolds, he signs himself off self-effacingly as 'your . . . coscribbler', and to his sister-in-law Georgiana he does not spare even his profoundest poetry from facetious comment: '[George] is making now [a copy] of an *Ode to the nightingale*, which is like reading an account of the black hole at Calcutta on an iceberg'.

Humour and high seriousness succeed each other briskly in Keats's letters, each mood being an essential element in the 'chameleon' disposition, the adaptable temperament, of Keats's ideal poet. In the midst of a strenuous engagement with a recalcitrant idea, which he is struggling to drag into the light of intelligent understanding, Keats is likely to drop a modest disclaimer which undercuts any tendency towards pretentiousness that such mental efforts might suggest: 'I am sometimes so very sceptical as to think poetry itself a mere jack-o'-lantern'. The philosophy that gradually unfolds in the letters is generally unsystematic, spontaneous, off-the-cuff and, as such, makes few claims for itself. Keats's remarks seem to materialise as the occasion arises, without much forethought: flashes of intuition not reason. He produces his pearls of insight like unconsidered trifles, having no intention of rough-hewing them into a philosophical system: they burst from his prose, like the wisdom of his verse, 'as naturally as leaves to a tree'. The beauty of Keats's speculations is that they are not organised and may well contradict one another: in the heart of such a rich disorder does the truth of Keats's poetic vision reside.

Though quietly confident in his poetical powers, Keats retained an inordinate modesty, often devaluing or dismissing a poem once his mind had ceased to work on it, as his letters show. His so-called miraculous year of poetic creation did not seem so miraculous to him, and he wrote to his brother George at the end of it: 'Nothing could have in all its circumstances fallen out worse for me than the last year has done, or could be more damping to my poetical talent'. The letters disclose an unconsciously ironic counterpoint between Keats's swift growth to spiritual maturity and his equally rapid physical decline: a dichotomy which finds expression in moments of mystified despondency and thoughts of suicide ('I am in that temper that if I were under water I would scarcely kick to come to the top').

On the whole the letters bear witness to Keats's remarkable resilience of spirit, which strove to turn all troubles and annoyances to account. Early on in his career he recognised that life's calamities, though 'like a nettle leaf or two in your bed', could act as a spur to greater creative endeavour, as if to defy 'the Devil himself'. 'I must think that difficulties nerve the spirit of a man', he wrote to Haydon in 1817, a conviction which formed the basis, in his letter to George two years later, of his perception of the world as a 'vale of soul-making' in which personal identity (or 'soul') is formed in direct response to the blows inflicted on it by life. The idea that suffering is an integral part of human experience, an indispensable ingredient in spiritual growth, was accepted by Keats in his letters well before it was assimilated into his poetry. At the same time (November 1817) that Endymion was shedding earthly sorrows and preparing, 'in a blissful swoon', for a perpetuity of ecstasy with his goddess, Keats was writing, more prosaically, but perhaps more profoundly, in a letter to Bailey: 'The first thing that strikes me on hearing a misfortune having befallen another is this. "Well, it cannot be helped. He will have the pleasure of trying the resources of his spirit"'.

Another item in Keats's philosophy to be engendered through the process of his letter-writing was his metaphor of life as a 'mansion of many apartments' (in the letter to Reynolds of 3 May 1818), whereby consciousness develops through three stages: the first is the 'infant or thoughtless chamber' where childhood impressions are accumulated, the second is the 'chamber of maiden-thought', a room full of light which coincides with 'the awakening of the thinking principle', and the third stage is the 'dark passages' leading from this chamber to a space beyond conventional distinctions between 'good and evil', where everything is enshrouded in 'mist'. This image accurately foreshadows the development of Keats's poetic philosophy, which ends indeterminately in the ambiguous vision of the death-pale Moneta in the 'cloudy' temple of 'The Fall of Hyperion'.

To the end of his life Keats's letters reveal insights into the nature of poetry, not only his own but all poetry. T. S. Eliot, who was not normally indulgent towards the Romantic temperament, said of the letters: 'There is hardly one statement of Keats about poetry, which . . . will not be found to be true'. Keats's last letter contains a definition of poetic ability, 'the knowledge of contrast, feeling for light and shade, all that information (primitive sense) necessary for a poem', which shows that Keats, dying with wasted lungs in a strange land, was still able to apply his mind to the contemplation of poetry and penetrate to a further understanding of it. Poetry and life nourished each other to the final moment.

2 KEATS'S POEMS:

SUMMARIES AND CRITICAL

COMMENTARIES

2.1 SONNETS

2.1.1 'On First Looking into Chapman's Homer'

Summary
The speaker recounts his varied reading experiences, all of them valuable but none so bracing as his first encounter with the Greek poet Homer, whose works he had often heard mentioned but never delved into until his discovery of an English translation of them by the Elizabethan poet George Chapman. The perusal of Homer has been a revelation, eclipsing all of the speaker's previous reading and exhilarating him with the Greek's clarity and breadth of vision. He sees himself, on this momentous occasion, in terms of an astronomer who locates a new, unlooked-for star in the firmament, or as a brazen conquistador standing dumbfounded on the threshold of a new, unsuspected ocean.

Commentary
The poem issued directly from Keats's experience, having been produced immediately after a visit to Charles Cowden Clarke's during which the volume of Chapman's Homer was studied. It has a standard Petrarchan structure, the octave (the first eight lines) preparing the ground for the moment of enlightenment revealed in the sestet (the last six lines). It is the first of Keats's sonnets to build to a proper climax and, as Leigh Hunt said, it 'completely announced the new poet taking possession'. The octave has a rather plodding rhythm with heavily accented iambic feet predominant ('And many góodlў státes and kingdoms séen') and a pause at the end of each line. Then in the sestet iambic regularity ceases to dominate: the move-ment of the verse becomes more flexible ('Whĕn ă néw plánĕt swíms into his Kĕn) and the sense overruns the line-endings ('with eagle eyes/He stared', 'all his men/Looked at each other'), to indicate the

excitement that succeeds to the reader's hitherto rather pedestrian progress.

The octave relates an experience that unfolds in time. The speaker's knowledge accumulates gradually as he unhurriedly voyages through one book after another. The adverbs of time, 'oft' and 'never', emphasise the slowness of the process. Then in the sestet the pace quickens and all considerations of time disappear, for the reading of Homer effects such a revolution in the speaker's thinking that it seems to happen out of the realm of time altogether. This is one of those epiphanies, those split seconds of intense awareness that flood the mind and soul with light, that Wordsworth categorised as 'spots of time': moments that burn so deeply into the consciousness that they seem to endure for ever.

The contrast in metre between the measured tranquillity of the octave and the erratic spontaneity of the seset is meant to enhance the theme, to emphasise what a break with the uneventful past the speaker's reading of Homer has accomplished. Temperate predictability has been replaced by flushed expectancy. The diction and images of the sonnet's two sections contribute further to this contrast. Literary experience is seen in the octave as something of lasting value ('gold'), though its acquisition does not involve much excitement. The images of the octave stress traditional hierarchical divisions between master and servant (or classical writer and modern reader) through the use of consciously archaic language such as 'bards', 'fealty' and 'demesne'. The concept of the present-day poet making an oath of loyalty ('fealty') to Apollo, the Greek god of poetry, is conventional rather than startlingly original (an 'Ode to Apollo' was among Keats's juvenile experiments in verse). Apollo does not have the symbolic resonance that Keats was to develop for him in later poems such as 'Hyperion'. He is a flat figure, a ready-to-hand stereotype for the source of inspiration. The keyword in setting the tone of the octave is 'goodly': reading the works of early authors is worthwhile without being particularly soul-stirring.

All is changed in the sestet: the 'goodly' assimilation of other men's learning has been replaced by 'wild' speculation. Two vivid similes illuminate the transformation. Gone is the octave's tone of deference, of acceptance of a limited, feudally-defined sphere of action. The horizontal gaze of the mariner has become the vertical scrutiny of the astronomer, peering into the skies as if to send mental probes 'to the very bourne of heaven' (Keats's phrase in *Endymion*). The classical temper of the octave gives way to the Romantic mood of the sestet; and it is paradoxically the primary classical poet Homer who has provided the stimulus for this new reading of the universe. The final image of the intrepid explorer speechless before the endless vista opened up beneath him is also a picture of the speaker, Keats himself, at the threshold of his poetic career, stunned into silence at the thought of all the new worlds he might possibly create: a task which, unblessed though he be, like the rugged buccaneer Cortez, by class distinction or social eminence, he does not balk from undertaking but rather anticipates with fierce, all-conquering 'eagle' eye. The poem both encapsulates Keats's development so far – the slow germination of his literary identity – and prophesies the as-yet unenvisioned achievements, the triumphs that are to come.

2.1.2 'On Sitting Down to Read *King Lear* Once Again'

Summary
The speaker declares his intention of resisting, for the nonce, the charms of romantic literature and grappling instead with a Shakespearean work which incorporates both romance and reality: a more arduous task, but one that may yield richer rewards. He then invokes both Shakespeare, as England's most soul-searching poet, and the atmosphere of England itself to sustain him in his self-appointed literary endeavour and to inspire him to new heights in his own writing, so that through the painful experience of immersing himself in *King Lear* he might be better equipped to tackle similarly disturbing subjects honestly, without looking for an escape route.

Commentary
The 'I' of the sonnet is again Keats himself, and the subject is once more the power exerted by books at the deepest level of his being. Reading Shakespeare's darkest tragedy is looked forward to as something of an ordeal, a trial by 'burning': a sentiment with which Samuel Johnson, so 'shocked' by Cordelia's death that he could not bear to reread *King Lear* for many years, would have concurred.

Fittingly, since Shakespeare is at the core of the poem's meditation, the sonnet blends Shakespearean and Petrarchan structures. There is not only a Petrarchan division between octave and sestet, but also a final couplet turning the poem in a more positive direction typical of the structure of many of Shakespeare's sonnets.

Keats is again using a poem to explore the nature of poetry. He here exhibits a dissatisfaction with romance not evident in the 'Chapman's Homer' sonnet. Written 15 months later (January 1818), the poem records a further stage in Keats's development as a poet. Now the 'serene' music that had galvanised his enthusiasm in the earlier sonnet seems somehow inadequate. The romantic version of life is persuasive ('golden-tongued') and alluring ('Syren'-like), but Keats knows that it can only retain its attractiveness by virtue of what it excludes, just as the heroic image of Cortez in the earlier poem had neglected (apart from an oblique reference to his predatory 'eagle eyes') the seedier aspects of the man. Romance offers a false paradise, like the Bower of Bliss in Spenser's *Faerie Queene*, and is

hence relegated to the realm of the past through the expressions
'Queen of far-away!' and 'Shut up thy olden pages'. Keats senses the
need for a more comprehensive view of life than that offered by pure
romanticism which, because of its selectivity, turns aside from life
instead of facing it. Such bold confrontation he knew he would find in
Shakespeare's *King Lear*.

King Lear, with its account of an old man moved by a sense of life's
spiritual significance ('impassioned clay') and rejected by his
daughters who deny it (bringing on themselves 'damnation'), offered
a world-view that combined both romantic and realistic elements: a
literary landscape towards which Keats was now reaching, as he had
earlier pledged in 'Sleep and Poetry' ('Where I may find the agonies,
the strife/Of human hearts'). *Endymion*, which he broke off revising
in order to reread *Lear* (and write this sonnet), contained too much
that was 'sweet' and not enough that was 'bitter'. The *King Lear*
sonnet renews Keats's dedication of himself to confront suffering and
find a place for it in his verse: a concern that preoccupied him for the
rest of his career. He had already outgrown the romantic belief in
perfectibility seemingly endorsed in *Endymion*. By the time he came
to revise that work for the press, it seemed based on 'a barren
dream'. Keats now realises that pain and suffering are integral to a
full view of life and are essential elements in any poetic composition
that claims to amplify its readers' understanding.

As in the 'Chapman's Homer' sonnet, Keats is looking both behind
and ahead. Having discarded the romantic excesses of *Endymion*,
like a snake shedding an old skin, Keats turns his back on his old
self – 'mute' now because in the presence of his new self it has
nothing useful to say – and prepares to enter a darker world where
sorrow and enlightenment are confusedly intertwined: the 'old oak
forest' of his next serious project, 'Hyperion'. The image of the
'Phoenix' emphasises the poet's present transitional state: like the
mythical bird he wants to set fire to his old self (the preface he
subsequently wrote to *Endymion* could be seen as such an act of
self-destruction) in the hope that a new one will rise from the ashes.
The poet is always on the point of becoming something else, 'tip-toe'
(as he says elsewhere) on the verge of a new experience and a fresh
identity, and the phoenix is only one among many images of
transition that abound in Keats's work.

2.1.3 'When I have fears that I may cease to be'

Summary
Premonitions of premature death visit the speaker intermittently,
troubling him with the thought that he might expire before the
accomplishment of his life's work – the shaping of the multitudinous
fancies and concepts that ebb and flow through his mind into clear

and concrete linguistic forms ('charactery') intelligible to the layman. At such times not only the abstract offspring of the brain but the physical presence of the human body seems insubstantial and liable to fade at any moment ('fair creature of an hour'), inducing in the speaker a state of unproductive inertia, since even the ideals he had hitherto thought worth striving for – love and fame – seem to promise at best a limited durability before being engulfed in the vortex that devours all material creations.

Commentary

This is the first of Keats's sonnets to be completely Shakespearean in form, with the first 12 lines piling up impressions and the couplet providing the counterweight or, as in this instance, the epitome. The poem's principal concern – its musing on the possibility of finding permanence in the midst of universal flux – also echoes a recurrent theme in Shakespeare's sonnets, though its outcome in 'nothingness' is less optimistic than Shakespeare, more particularly Keatsian.

The sonnet was written at the same time as the *King Lear* sonnet (January 1818) and reflects Keats's absorption at this time in his 'Presider', Shakespeare, while simultaneously indicating a depressive streak in Keats – what he called a 'morbidity of temperament' – that is not discernible in his precursor. Prospero's visions in *The Tempest* may be built of a 'fabric' that is without foundation ('baseless'), but there is no sense that all might be vanity, illusions constructed in a godless void. Keats's anxieties proceed from an inability to accept Christian truths on trust: the only 'truth' he knows is that which issues from the imagination. 'Cease to be' envisages no postmortal existence, merely the loss of sensibility after death prognosticated in 'Ode to a Nightingale'.

Keats's agnosticism explains why these fits of depression should so immobilise him. The menace of death's arbitrary inteference is sufficient to paralyse the poet's creative urge and make him abandon his heroic goal. On the other hand, to harvest the products of his imagination is by now, as he knows, a task about whose performance there is really no choice: his brain is 'teeming' and must be assisted in delivering its progeny. Poetry writing is a natural process, occurring almost spontaneously through 'the magic hand of chance'. The conflict expressed here, at this pause in Keats's career between finishing *Endymion* and beginning 'Isabella' (probably the 'high romance' referred to) while preparing for the bigger undertaking of 'Hyperion', is the struggle between hope and despair, between the impulsion towards Herculean labours of preparation and production and the temptation to despondency, sloth and inertia. From the flood of subsequent works, it was evidently the Apollonian Keats – whose 'lyre shall never have a slackened string' ('Apollo to the Graces') – that won the day over the Keats tempted to succumb passively to the sweet siren songs of hopeless leisure, 'content to stoop' and accept defeat like the fallen Titan, Oceanus, in 'Hyperion'.

Through the negative colouring of the sonnet one of Keats's mature perceptions about poetry is already gleaming through: its altruistic quality. Keats came to realise that, unlike human relationships, the relationship between art and the individual reader or viewer, between giver and receiver, could not be reciprocal. The lonely figure of Moneta in 'The Fall of Hyperion' 'comforts those she sees not', just as Keats in this earlier poem 'stands alone', acknowledging that the works he hopes to harvest from his brain before his death will be left behind, like grain stored in barns, for unknown others to feed upon.

2.1.4 'Bright star! would I were steadfast as thou art'

Summary
The speaker rejects the idea that he might ever attain the state of serene indifference, of objectivity, that the star he looks at seems to embody: an immobile state superior to the emotional changeability of human beings while still exerting a beneficent influence on their environment. The sort of permanence he rather seeks is a more limited, less public one: an eternal sedation in the arms of his beloved from which only death will remove him.

Commentary
The sonnet has a Shakespearean format (three quatrains, or four-lined rhyming units, and a couplet) superimposed on a basically Petrarchan structure of octave and sestet, with the shift of focus coming in line 9. This shift of focus – from a cosmic panorama that encompasses the whole planet with its seas, shores, mountains, moors and neighbouring stars, to a claustrophobic imprisonment in the fair one's embrace – is signalled by the ironic repetition of the word 'steadfast' which, in the sestet, has a diminished, purely physical sense in place of the allusions to spiritual constancy that irradiate it in the octave. The sonnet, in other words, spirals down to end in anti-climax, displaying as it does so Keats's degeneration from the nobly-conceived role of impersonal poet 'pouring out a balm upon the world' (Moneta's definition of him in 'The Fall of Hyperion') to a state of animal insensibility, a captive of his carnal nature.

There is some dispute as to the date of composition, but the majority opinion seems to favour late autumn 1819 as the most likely date and Fanny Brawne as the most probable addressee (she copied it into an edition of Dante that Keats had given her). The poem discloses the conflict between poetic duty and surrender to the mastery of love. The octave, with its image of the star glowing with spiritual light in the course of its performance of its responsibilities, its guidance and 'watching' unsleepingly over the behaviour of lower essences, conveys the altruistic aim of the dedicated poet who foregoes a personal life in order to be an 'Eremite', a recluse who will provide sustenance to his fellows in consequence of his self-sacrifice. The star/poet's duty is linked to the cleansing activity of the waters, whose task is similarly 'priestlike', solemn and self-denying. But this is a role which Keats has already renounced: he is determined that 'Not in lone splendour' will he shine. In the battle between poetry and the pulsing blood the latter is winning; and in the sestet the poet falls from the heavens in a 'swoon' on his beloved's breast, in an attitude that mocks the very meaning of 'steadfastness'.

The fainting posture recalls the state of 'indolence' – the halfway stage to true poetry before the imaginative energy from the 'bright star' of consciousness has been brought to bear on the mind's manifold impressions – that has often tempted the poet in his career. Fittingly the poem terminates in 'death', since the choice that has been made in it spells the end of the speaker's poetic identity, even though his personal one may continue. He seems aware that guilt will remind him of the cowardice of his choice in his prophecy of the 'sweet unrest' that will disturb his repose on his true love's bosom. The mingling of filial and amorous sensations in 'Pillowed upon my fair love's ripening breast' is a further acknowledgement that the poet has abdicated his rule and his role as a responsible artist and regressed to a state of childhood unthinkingness – he wishes 'to feel for ever', perhaps to think never again.

The sonnet announces Keats's retirement from the lists of poetic challenge, whose gauntlet he had taken up so enthusiastically in the 'Chapman's Homer' sonnet. He, like Glaucus in *Endymion*, has yielded to his Circe, and the noble image of tenacity, resolution and illumination contained in the bright star is conjured in farewell to what might have been. It is Keats's passing tribute to the poetic self that has been sabotaged by the personal self, an apology for fecklessness, as he confesses in the first line: 'Bright star! would I were steadfast as thou art'. It must be remembered, though, that such regressions were familiar interludes in Keats's poetic career, usually appearing in the trough of a wave of great creative energy, between major poems (see 'When I have fears' above). Had Keats's health not failed him shortly afterwards, it is likely that the mood of capitulation of the 'Bright star' sonnet would have proved as transient as it had done on previous occasions and Keats's usual resilience would have reasserted itself.

2.2 NARRATIVE POEMS

2.2.1 *Endymion*

Summary
Endymion, a gentleman shepherd on the slopes of Mount Latmos in Greece, is embraced in his sleep by Cynthia, the moon-goddess. Unaware of her identity, but realising that she is not entirely of this world – perhaps a 'maid of the waters' or 'a nymph of Dian's', he conjectures (II, 690–2) – he spends his waking hours in fruitless search for her. This is the story that he relates to his sister Peona in Book I, after she has questioned him on the cause of his melancholy.

In Book II Endymion is drawn into the dark underworld, 'the silent mysteries of earth' (214), where he follows voices and discovers a brilliant light in the heart of the cavern ('an orbèd diamond, set to fray/Old darkness from his throne': 245–6). He encounters another pairing of mortal with immortal, Adonis and Venus, prefiguring a happy conclusion to his own affair. A further fleeting visit from his heavenly paramour, 'Fondling and kissing every doubt away' (735), seems to promise the same result.

In Book III Endymion's environment changes from the subterranean to the subaqueous. He continues his wanderings under the ocean, where he meets the old man Glaucus, who tells him how his beloved Scylla was frozen in death by the enchantress Circe. With the assistance of Endymion Glaucus is not only released from Circe's spell and rejuvenated, but empowered to reanimate Scylla and all other lovers drowned at sea. This general resurrection is celebrated by a 'glorious revelry' (924) at Neptune's palace. Endymion alone is without his partner at this festival, but his 'inward senses' receive an ethereal message from his elusive love: 'Immortal bliss for me too hast thou won' (1020–4).

Instead of this promise being fulfilled at the start of Book IV, however, Endymion is sidetracked into an affair with an Indian maid. Upon meeting her Endymion decides to devote himself to the sensual pleasure that she seems to promise, and declares his renunciation of the 'cloudy phantasms' (651) of his supramundane love. At one point he loses both earthly and heavenly mistresses, and undergoes a stupefied penance in the 'Cave of Quietude' (548). Finally, at the end of his trials, the Indian maid changes into Cynthia – 'in her eyes a brighter day/Dawned blue and full of love' (985–6) - and Endymion, effectively 'spiritualised' (993) by all his suffering, is permitted to 'vanish' with her, leaving his sister in the 'gloomy wood' to ponder on these events.

Commentary

In *Endymion*, written between April and November 1817, Keats
flexed his intellectual muscles, taking some rather flimsy material
from Greek myth and attempting to expand it to the dimensions of an
epic. He regarded the sustained narrative form of the epic as the
sternest test of the poet's ability. Composed in loosely-constructed
couplets which encouraged an undisciplined, run-on manner of
delivery, the poem invites allegorical interpretations; but its rambling
structure and glaring inconsistencies (the Indian maid, for instance,
gives three contradictory reasons for her concealment of her true
identity: IV, 989–93) thwart any comprehensive allegorical reading.
Generally, it can be said to explore the conflict in the Romantic poet
between the desire to pursue noble ideals (Cynthia) and the need to
satisfy his own hedonistic urges. Endymion's bifurcated libido directs
him ('O state perplexing!': IV, 439) both upwards to the moon-
goddess ('His heart leapt up as to its rightful throne': IV, 445) and
downwards to the Indian maid ('so beauteous was his bed-fellow,/He
could not help but kiss her': IV, 448–9). Keats probably intended to
indicate by this that the energies common to both creation (poetry)
and procreation (sex) are a blend of the physical and the 'ethereal',
and that one cannot achieve elevation to the higher sphere without
having undergone a certain amount of degradation in the lower.
Suffering, despair, even the bestial transformation that Endymion's
alter ego, Glaucus, suffers are all necessary experiences on the road
to attainment of the ideal.

Many readers and critics have found Keats's dramatisation of this
theme – the education of the soul through suffering and experience – to be imprecise or arbitrary in *Endymion*. Despite its
immaturity, though, the poem introduces ideas and techniques that
occur, more finely honed, in Keats's later work. The fecundity of
nature, for instance, which overflows from the first stanza of 'To
Autumn', is indicated in Book I of *Endymion* ('the dairy pails/Bring
home increase of milk': 44–5), together with the idea of the younger
generation continually replenishing – or, as in 'Hyperion', replac-
ing – the older one ('the early budders are just new,/And run in
mazes of the youngest hue/About old forests': 41–3). In the initial
idyllic Arcadian scenes man and nature sing the same song.

Endymion's early idealism, tempered by his subsequent adven-
tures, is summarised in the 'fellowship with essence' speech (I,
777–842). Keats glossed this idea in a letter to his publisher as 'a kind
of pleasure thermometer' by which the individual is led through joy in
natural phenomena, then pleasure in music and poetry, to friendship
and love, becoming progressively more spiritual, the ultimate goal in
Endymion being to progress – through 'a sort of oneness . . . like a
floating spirit's' – up to eventual 'fellowship divine,/A fellowship
with essence', when the acolyte has presumably discarded all his

earthly attributes and become angelic. The giddiness of such a euphoric state was understood by Keats, which is why Endymion subsequently undergoes so many shocks and disappointments before he is granted his goal. Poetic inspiration can lead to 'madness' (II, 218) if the poet forgets his own humanity, loses his earthly ballast and floats free of gravitation and all human anchorage. So Endymion plunges into the earth, the 'voice' (II, 200) from the cavern (perhaps of his unconscious) warning him to counteract his aerial inclinations by recognising what is earthy about him. Willingly or not, Endymion is forced to explore his own clayey heritage, even if in so doing the heaven he aspires to threatens to recede altogether beyond his grasp the further he 'descends'. Eventually he is forced to recognise that he is neither god nor ghost – simply 'an exiled mortal' (II, 316).

The Glaucus episode teaches Endymion about the bonds of sympathy that tie him to his species. His meeting with Glaucus tutors some of his own nascent humanity: 'his heart gan warm/With pity' (III, 282–3). For his personal salvation Endymion needs the intercession of the Indian maid. Ironically, he is 'spiritualised' by becoming earthlier; he becomes a god by behaving as humanly as possible in the course of his tests.

In *Endymion* Keats, in his own words, 'leaped headlong into the sea'. Like Glaucus, he plunged into a strange and fearsome element – the English poetic tradition – and strained to 'interknit' his 'senses with so dense a breathing stuff' (III, 380–1). The poem created its own truths as it went along ('That which is creative must create itself', said Keats), making its discoveries at the same time that they were made by its hero. Thus if it is an allegory it is a spontaneous and pragmatic one, not the 'continued allegory' of Spenser's *Faerie Queene*. This is the technique of all of Keats's major poetry: beauty and truth unfold themselves to writer and reader alike, opening themselves up unexpectedly in the course of a mainly unmapped journey.

2.2.2 'Isabella' or 'The Pot of Basil'

Summary
Set in medieval Florence, the story tells of the love of the unassuming Lorenzo for the equally bashful Isabella, the sister of his employers. The affair is detected by Isabella's two brothers, who had intended to enrich themselves further by marrying her 'To some high noble and his olive-trees'. Jealously incensed by their factor's presumption in courting their sister, they trick him into riding off with them 'Into a forest quiet for the slaughter'. Having murdered Lorenzo there, they return to tell Isabella that sudden business has necessitated Lorenzo's precipitate departure 'for foreign lands'. Saddened by the absence of her lover, Isabella suspects nothing worse until she is visited some

time afterwards by Lorenzo's ghost, which unravels the 'horrid' plot and tells her where his grave might be found. Isabella locates the grave and disinters her beloved's body. She cuts the head from it, takes it home and conceals it in a 'garden-pot' in which a basil plant is set to grow. Inconsolable for her loss, Isabella secludes herself with the plant, scarcely bothering to attend to her spiritual or physical needs ('seldom did she go to chapel-shrift,/And seldom felt she any hunger-pain'). Perturbed by their sister's acute melancholia, the brothers trace the source to the basil pot, which they 'examine . . . in secret place', coming face to face with the victim of their crime, their 'murdered man'. Horrified, they flee the country, leaving their sister to die a 'forlorn' death and the basil plant to live on in Italian legend.

Commentary
Based on a fourteenth-century story by the Italian Giovanni Boccaccio, and written in March and April 1818, 'Isabella' still shows signs of Keats's immaturity, although it does not expose its defects in the artlessly effusive manner of *Endymion*. This time Keats used the Italian *ottava rima* (eight-line verses rhyming *abababcc*), disciplining himself to present the story stanza by stanza, in a series of tableaux.

'Isabella' deploys an uncomfortable mixture of tones. Trying to display the maturity and worldly wisdom so conspicuously absent from *Endymion*, Keats sometimes attempts to inject the urbane scepticism of Byron into his poem ('Too many tears for lovers have been shed,/Too many sighs give we to them in fee'). Such an attitude does not blend easily with the compassion for the lovers that comes more naturally to Keats ('So sweet Isabel,/By gradual decay from beauty fell,/Because Lorenzo came not'). There is not one constant point of view, one steady perspective upon the lovers, who keep approaching and withdrawing from the reader as Keats adjusts the focus from sympathy to detachment and back again. The characters are too naïve and one-dimensional to be wholly dignified: the innocent ignorance of 'poor simple Isabel!' is matched by the uninformed gaucherie of 'Lorenzo, a young palmer in Love's eye!' The two lovers are passive and ductile, fit only to 'dream and nightly weep', and their mutual passion seems initially as much an illness as a blessing: 'some stir of heart, some malady'.

There is, however, some psychologicical exactness in the depiction of each lover's obsession with the other. Isabel 'spoilt her half-done broidery' by unwittingly introducing Lorenzo's name into the pattern, and his sleepless nights are given a specific intensity that takes them beyond cliché: habitually he would 'with sick longing all the night outwear,/To hear her morning-step upon the stair'. When love is belatedly declared, it is Isabella who takes the initiative ('in her tone and look he read the rest'). The 'sweet' that ensues does not come without 'bitterness': it is impossible to savour the one without first digesting the other. Pleasure and knowledge can only come after pain and suffering, an idea that was becoming a central tenet of Keats's philosophy: 'bees . . . Know there is richest juice in poison-flowers'.

In contrast to the 'richest juice' enjoyed by Lorenzo and Isabella, which is at least partly spiritual (his lips that 'poesied with hers in dewy rhyme' suggest both kisses and the more refined delights of expressing love-sentiments), it is greed alone that fills Isabella's brothers. The 'rich-ored driftings of the flood' can only be secured by enslaving others – 'for them . . . many once proud-quivered loins did melt/In blood from stinging whip' – and degrading life, debasing it instead of elevating it. Keats makes the contrast between material and spiritual wealth – between making profits and making poe-try – explicit: 'Why were they proud? Because red-lined accounts/Were richer than the songs of Grecian years?' The two sorts of wealth are concentrated in the word 'richer', and the 'red-lined' accounts suggest not only the red ink but the shed blood – the sin against humanity – that is inseparable from such nefarious commercial en-terprise.

The innocence of the lovers seems doomed in this world of 'torchèd mines', 'noisy factories' and 'ship-mast forests' where the ducat is ruler. In such an environment the love which had promised to bear fruit ('Grew, like a lusty flower') is inevitably stillborn, leaving a sense of pity for the beauty that the world destroys: 'there was striving, in its piteous tongue,/To speak as when on earth it was awake,/And Isabella on its music hung'. The unfulfilled nature of this love is poignantly stressed in a stark tactile image, when Isabella puts the glove from Lorenzo's grave 'in her bosom', where 'it dries/And freezes utterly unto the bone/Those dainties made to still an infant's cries'. The child promised by the 'lusty flower' of their passion will never be made; mother's milk will never emerge from Isabella's chilled breasts.

The poem's pathos, its failure to make the deep impression produced by tragedy's complex interweaving of light and dark filaments, was recognised at once as a defect by Keats, always his own severest critic. '"Isabella" is what I should call, were I a reviewer, "a weak-sided poem" with an amusing sober-sadness about it', he told Woodhouse. He had even begun his strictures on it within the poem itself: 'Ah! wherefore all this wormy circumstance?/Why linger at the yawning tomb so long?' he reprimanded himself in the forty-ninth stanza. Yet 'Isabella' does carry, in embryo, a conception that was to see the light of day in Keats's later poems: his realisation that romantic poetry should not simply offer an escape but must contain, too, the suffering of the real world. The poem offers the consolation that beauty – even though it be 'Beauty that must die' ('Ode on Melancholy') – can be found in the midst of horror. The balanced view of life towards which Keats was struggling must include both beauty and horror, as Shakespeare's tragedies did. Both are contained in the basil pot, where the 'fast mouldering head' that is 'vile with green and livid spot' is watered by the loving 'tears' into which Isabella pours what remains of her beauty. The basil pot is a precursor of the Grecian urn, where disparate elements of savagery and civility, sound and silence, are held together in a more perfect equipoise.

2.2.3 'Hyperion'

Summary

Book I begins with the god Saturn, leader of the Titans, sitting 'unsceptred' in apathetic despondency and musing on the reasons for his recent defeat at the hands of the new generation of gods led by his son Jupiter. Saturn is commiserated by Thea, a female deity and fellow sufferer. Her presence eventually rouses him to thoughts of revenge and he pledges himself to a counter-revolution which will put his upstart Olympian offspring, 'the rebel three', back in their place (I, 147). Cheered by Saturn's recovery of confidence, Thea leads him to the 'covert' whither the other 'fallen' gods have withdrawn. Meanwhile one Titan remains undeposed on his throne: Hyperion, god of the sun. Unsettled by the strange and bitter odours he inhales from his earthly altars, Hyperion becomes irascible and insomniac. Having seen visions of his own imminent fall from power, he vows to resist the rebels and to aid Saturn in recovering 'his throne again'. His own parent Coelus, himself a superannuated god since the inception of Saturn's reign and imperfectly understanding the nature of the present conflict, encourages Hyperion in his resolve.

In Book II Saturn and Thea discover the other Titans sprawled listlessly in a gloomy landscape of rocks and cataracts. Saturn upbraids them for their defeatism and a debate ensues. Oceanus, 'God of the Sea' (167), counsels acceptance of the new dispensation, seeing it as historically inevitable: just as the Titans themselves had ousted the earlier regime of 'old Darkness', so 'on our heels a fresh perfection treads' (212)A. His argument is supported by his daughter Clymene, who describes how the music of the Olympians utterly surpasses, in its 'new blissful golden melody' (280), the 'dull' songs of the Titans. A new cosmic harmony has evolved, it seems, and it would be folly to resist it. The trend of capitulation provokes a strong reaction from 'huge Enceladus', who contemptuously dismisses the arguments of the two previous speakers and shames his audience into showing a more vigorous response. As if to second this call to action,

Hyperion appears 'in midst of his own brightness' (373); but his obvious lowness of spirits soon plunges the Titans back into 'despondence', while Saturn's face displays 'no joy'.

Book III switches to a lusher landscape where Hyperion's replacement, Apollo, the new god of the sun, roams 'ankle-deep in lilies of the vale' (35). He is in the process of assuming his godhead, a painful and mystifying experience akin to rebirth. To help him through it he is attended by Mnemosyne (or memory), the mother of the muses, a Titaness who has changed sides, she says, 'for the sake/Of loveliness new born' (78–9). As Apollo is engulfed in the throes of shedding his mortal nature, the poem breaks off.

Commentary

Having learnt from *Endymion* to be more disciplined and dispassionate, Keats set about composing 'Hyperion' with a firmer intellectual grip, 'in a more naked and Grecian manner', as he said. The use of blank verse freed him from what Milton called 'the bondage of rhyming', but it inevitably echoed its monumental precursor *Paradise Lost* (the debate in Book II is particularly reminiscent of the debate of the rebel angels in Book II of Milton's epic), and he eventually abandoned it because, as he said to Reynolds, 'there were too many Miltonic inversions in it'. The bulk of it was written between September and December 1818. It is the first production of his 'miraculous year', and he returned to tinker with it from time to time, finally recasting it as 'The fall of Hyperion', also unfinished. Keats intended to exercise rigorous control over its material, purging it of the luxuries and excrescences of *Endymion*, so that it would advance in a clear narrative line in which 'the march of passion and endeavour will be undeviating'.

Keats again turned to Greek legend to embody his theme. This time it was the war of succession among the gods, a myth embellished and altered by Keats and one whose later incidents, had he completed his plan, would, in the words of Woodhouse, 'have been pure creations of the poet's brain'. Keats adapted the classical story to become the vehicle for the theme of spiritual evolution, of growth through suffering.

Initially the fallen Saturn, 'quiet as a stone', infects the environment, which takes its colour from his numbed immobility: 'By reason of his fallen divinity/Spreading a shade' (I, 12–13). The scene has the still quality of painting, or of sculpture – 'the Naiad 'mid her reeds/Pressed her cold finger closer to her lips' – while retaining the potential for movement. Nature is willing to sympathise for a while with 'fallen divinity', but sooner or later it must transfer its allegiance to a new generation of gods – the Olympians – in accordance with the evolutionary principles endorsed by the poem. The 'once serene domain' of the Saturnian Golden Age must perforce bow to the inevitable. Perhaps serenity teaches no lessons, steels no souls.

Unlike nature, however, the Titans are for the most part incapable of adaptation to new circumstances, and must be pensioned off into sedentary subsidiary roles ('he went into his quiet cave/To muse for ever', says Keats of the Titan 'Oceanus the old' in *Endymion*, III, 994), because of their failure to admit the notion of progress. The arrival of the dynamic Apollo gives the statuesque Titans no more capacity for action than pieces in a museum.

The static disarray of the Titans, as if they have been smitten by a great force and rendered useless, is conveyed in images that link them with ancient prehistory, isolation, coldness, obscurity and insensibility:

> Scarce images of life, one here, one there,
> Lay vast and edgeways; like a dismal cirque
> Of Druid stones, upon a forlorn moor.
>
> (II, 33–5)

They no longer have any communal role to play, but are discarded as the gods of yesterday upon the appearance of a new set of symbols around which man may organise his life's energies.

The 'vale' in which Saturn and Thea find themselves is the 'vale of soul-making' (of Keats's letter to George, 14 February 1819) where they suffer pain: 'Though an immortal, she felt cruel pain' (I, 44). But the Titans cannot learn the lesson of suffering, and they respond to it with anger instead of understanding. 'I will advance a terrible right arm/Shall scare that infant thunderer, rebel Jove', fumes Hyperion (I, 248–9). He envisages fighting a rearguard right-wing action, intending to re-establish the old order rather than accommodate the new, just as Saturn dreams of repeating, without modification, his earlier creation of an ordered universe: 'Where is another Chaos?' (I, 145). The Golden Age, so beloved of the eighteenth-century Augustans for its calm serenity, is rejected in the Romantic age. There is no place for Saturn's mild despotism in the 'fierce convulse' (III, 129) of the Apollonian era.

Apollo becomes divine by activating the god in man, particularly through exploiting the poetic faculty. The music he creates on his 'golden bow' while still a mortal is a symbolic foreshadowing of this realisation, using as it does physical instruments and sounds to sketch the outline of a spiritual perfection – using time to measure a harmony that is beyond time, and thus seeming to reach the ear both consecutively and simultaneously:

> Each family of rapturous hurried notes,
> That fell, one after one, yet all at once,

Like pearl beads dropping sudden from their string.
                                    (II, 282–4)

As elsewhere in Keats, the worst and darkest moment for Apollo
('dark, dark,/And painful vile oblivion seals my eyes': III, 86–7) is
that which precedes the breakthrough to an extended awareness
('Knowledge enormous makes a God of me': III, 113). Suffering,
Keats had come to recognise, was the basis of wisdom; out of its
acknowledged weakness emerged the strength of the poetic vision.
Such a source of beauty was not available to the earlier, non-human
gods, the monumental Titans. He wrote to Reynolds (on 3 May
1818), 'Until we are sick, we understand not; in fine, as Byron says,
"knowledge is sorrow", and I go on to say that "sorrow is wisdom" '
The ingestion of such sorrow renders the sufferer almost impersonal,
objective in his understanding, and Apollo's face assumes a look of
detached emotionlessness, the expression of his 'gloomless' eyes only
recorded by what is *not* in them, as this knowledge is born within
him.

Titan and Olympian, Hyperion and Apollo, may represent the old
and the new Keats respectively. Apollo, apotheosised through pain,
might represent the new Keats who was learning to accommodate
suffering within his vision of the garden of sensual delights, while the
neurotic Hyperion reflects the immature Keats ever prone to attacks
from his 'morbidity of temperament'. The poem, in other words,
expresses Keats's transition into a more complete poet, a 'celestial'
one like Apollo with a viewpoint that embraced sorrow as well as joy.
Once the transformation was accomplished, there was no need for
the poem to continue.

2.2.4 'The Eve of St Agnes'

Summary
In the middle of winter an old beadsman is preparing to do penance,
sitting among ashes in the basement of a castle whose main apartments are given over to raucous celebration. The daughter of the
house, Madeline, is keyed up with anticipation, because this is St
Agnes' Eve (21 January) when, according to legend, 'young virgins'
will, if they fast and perform other 'ceremonies due', have visions of
their 'loves', and even a dream experience of the act of love itself,
'Upon the honeyed middle of the night'. Madeline's young admirer,
Porphyro, though detested by Madeline's family ('Whose very dogs
would execrations howl/Against his lineage'), has gained entrance to
the castle and, with the connivance of Madeline's aged maid-servant
Angela, has secreted himself into a closet adjacent to Madeline's
bedchamber. From here, intending initially to 'gaze and worship all
unseen', he watches his beloved undress and go to bed where, in 'the

poppied warmth of sleep', she expects St Agnes to fulfil the legend and introduce her dream lover to her sleeping self.

At this point Porphyro's ambitions mount higher. He creeps forth from his hiding place, bringing with him a luscious 'heap' of comestibles which he places beside Madeline's bed on 'lustrous salvers'. Accompanying himself on the lute, he gently awakens Madeline by singing an old Provençal song. Drowsily, Madeline perceives beside her the face she had been communing with in her dream, but remarks an alteration in it ('How changed thou art! How pallid, chill, and drear!'). The declaration of love that his somnolent mistress offers him spurs Porphyro's ambition to new heights so that, taking advantage of Madeline's semiconscious state, he consummates his passion without more ado, in 'solution sweet'.

Fully aroused to the reality of the situation, Madeline sees herself as 'a deceivèd thing – /A dove forlorn', but Porphyro, declaring himself her 'pilgrim', swears that his intentions are as pure as ever and offers to take her to a home he has prepared for her in warmer climes, across 'the southern moors'. Though 'beset with fears', Madeline consents to go with him. 'Like phantoms' the two lovers navigate their passage through 'be-nightmared' kinsmen, drunken retainers and watchful bloodhounds, effecting their escape and vanishing 'into the storm'. The same night both Angela and the beadsman die in ignominy and isolation.

Commentary

Keats wrote the poem in January and February 1819, probably from an idea suggested to him by a lady friend, Mrs Isabella Jones. The happy outcome of the events may have been projected from his wishes *vis à vis* Fanny Brawne, while a visit he made to Chichester at this time undoubtedly contributed to the poem's medieval atmosphere. It has a compactness and unity missing from his earlier romance narratives. The tone throughout is confidently knowledgeable without ever being cynical or condescending. Porphyro's opportunism attracts no wry comments, but is simply portrayed as the natural outcome of events (Keats told his publisher, who was aghast at the premarital coupling of the protagonists, that he 'should despise a man who would be such an eunuch . . . as to leave a maid, with that character about her, in such a situation'). The sexual realism is one of the fruits of Keats's maturity, a by-product of his determination to expunge naïvety from his poetry and not to leave himself open to the charge of 'inexperience of life' or 'simplicity of knowledge'.

The variety of his reading also coalesces in this poem to form an organic whole. While Spenser and Chatterton contribute to the medieval atmosphere, Shakespeare's *Romeo and Juliet* provides both the theme of two lovers encircled by hostile clansmen and the language of religious devotion applied to an earthly mistress: 'Ah, silver shrine, here will I take my rest', says Porphyro, echoing Romeo's reference to Juliet as a 'holy shrine' (I, v, 93). Nor is Milton, whose influence Keats had felt to be so overbearing in 'Hyperion', entirely absent from this poem: his technique of repetition, for instance, may be detected in

> They glide, like phantoms, into the wide hall;
> Like phantoms, to the iron porch they glide.

Yet none of these influences obtrudes; from beginning to end the poem speaks in a single controlled voice of quiet ebullience that is uniquely Keatsian.

All the contraries of life and death, joy and pain are absorbed in the lovers' triumphant consummation. Yet the climax retains an ambiguity that has provoked a wealth of critical comment. Have the lovers been able, through the sexual act, to transcend their physical bodies and rise to a metaphysical, immortal state of being, much like the 'vanishing' act of Endymion, 'spiritualised' by his trials? This is the line that the critic Earl R. Wasserman takes. Jack Stillinger, on the other hand, treats the poem more mundanely as a sort of verse-novel, whereby Porphyro, stripped of all spiritual pretension, becomes merely a 'peeping Tom and villainous seducer'. Keats has allowed the reader to write his own conclusion to the story by dispatching his lovers into a 'storm'. Is this tempest 'of haggard seeming' or 'a boon indeed'? Does it bless or curse, welcome or reject, those who fly into it? Does it signify the disintegration of the mortal body prior to its elevation to an immortal sphere, or is it simply the punishment that the lovers invite for their precipitate and unsanctioned behaviour? The open-ended conclusion – in which the lovers are 'phantoms' for whom doors slide open with miraculous ease while at the same time the watchdog responds to them as physical beings – invites endless speculation. What follows is just one of the many possible interpretations.

The presence of death, which frames the whole work, is palpable throughout the poem. Death lies like a yawning gulf beneath the surface of the poem's events. Porphyro and Madeline skate across the 'frozen' landscape of the setting, but at any moment the ice may crack and death swallow them. The omnipresence of death is manifest even in what is usually a sign of life – breath itself. The beadsman's breath, in the first stanza, 'seemed taking flight for heaven'. The normal barriers separating the living from the dead seem inoperable, with the 'sculptured dead' seeming to suffer ('Emprisoned in black, purgatorial rails') as much as the frozen living, at least in the imagination of the beadsman, who compassionates their discomfort ('To think how they may ache in icy hoods and mails'). In the midst of so much imagery of coldness the warm passion, suffused with blood-red 'gules' colour, of hero and heroine blooms exultantly if briefly. There is the suggestion that love and beauty may transcend, even reverse, the laws of time: 'As though a rose should shut and be a bud again'.

The human qualities that shine out in the midst of darkness, coldness and enmity are dwelled upon more than is the wickedness of the 'bloodthirsty race' of the Baron, thereby reducing the hostile elements to a harmless threat, like the decorative background of a tapestry (Keats himself applied the word 'drapery' to the poem), and ensuring that although the poem begins and ends with images of death, death does not bear the ultimate victory. The triumph of the good over the wicked, even though purchased at some pain (the beadsman's final penance in 'rough ashes', the 'palsied' demise of old Angela), ensures that the poem's tone is not tragic but rather a combination of medieval romance and Christian *memento mori*. The dominant impression the poem leaves is that life is a temporary condition whose termination is to be endured but not deplored. A warm spiritual zone – perhaps that to which the lovers have 'fled' – coexists alongside the inhospitable physical one that maims ('the hare limped') and benumbs ('silent was the flock') its inhabitants.

The sexual centre of the poem, where Porphyro 'blends' with Madeline, is also its thematic centre. The sexual act is the node at which the physical and spiritual planes meet, and, when performed in the spirit of loving devotion ('Thou art my heaven, and I thine eremite'), it becomes a sacramental act, simultaneously self-fulfilling and self-sacrificing, sensual and solemn both at once. Porphyro is trapped by his human nature into doing more than he had originally purposed – 'Perchance speak, kneel, touch, kiss' (although the progressively physical tendency of these verbs shows which way his instincts are driving). His surrender to his baser self, however, is redeemed by the love which he bears for Madeline and to whose dictates he remains subservient. The sexual act transforms Porphyro and Madeline, two individuals, into a corporate being, a spiritual entity able to 'glide' through all material obstacles.

The bass note to the treble of the 'argent revelry' and 'silver trumpets' that prevents this from being merely a 'faery' romance is provided by suggestions of the proximity of pain to the pleasures of love: 'As though a tongueless nightingale should swell/Her throat in vain, and die, heart-stifled, in her dell'. This simile, with its glance at the Philomela legend (in Greek myth Philomela was raped and rendered mute by her brother-in-law Tereus, and was subsequently transformed into a nightingale), is a reminder that, viewed in a certain light, Porphyro's conduct is that of a rapist (an impression reinforced by his stealthy approach to Madeline's bed, 'Noiseless as fear in a wide wilderness'). Cruelty towards the beloved is not entirely excluded from the lover's armoury (a point made more explicitly in 'Lamia'). Other reminders of savagery emerge through the references to 'dwarfish Hildebrand' and his ilk, 'more fanged than wolves and bears'. Keats's mature vision insists on the inclusion of the 'dark' truths of life, even in the pages of a romance. Nevertheless, the poem's Spenserian stanzas (units of nine lines, each of five iambic feet except for a final six-foot line, and rhyming *ababbcbcc*), the final Alexandrines (the elongated ultimate lines) of which help to stabilise each one by arresting its flowing movement, ensure that the narrative advances in a series of tableaux rather than in a continuous dynamic line; and this serves to assure the reader that the dark elements will never transcend their role of picturesque and ultimately impotent evil.

At the end Porphyro and Madeline have taken flight and death resumes its dominion. Their story might thus have been merely an interlude framed by the two 'meagre' admonitory older figures – an illusory and temporary escape from life's harsh, chilling realities only possible at their particular age. Having met and 'melted' into each other, they have reached the climax of their lives and will perhaps sunder, and certainly die, in the 'storm' of after years. The emphasis on time – 'ay, ages long ago' – in the last stanza perhaps bears witness to the temporal limitations of Porphyro's 'vassalage' to his 'lovely bride'. Their affair has the quality of an idyll, one which may be read, from the vantage point of age and experience, with the same sort of nostalgic condescension that Angela bestows upon it.

It is the one poem, however, in which the imagination is unconditionally victorious. Madeline and Porphyro do shake off their bonds, leave the warped and sterile physical world and fly to a warmer 'southern' land, a spiritual world whither neither Keats nor his readers may follow, but where, it is hoped, beauty and truth will shine upon them. Despite Keats's customary depreciation of his work (he valued 'St Agnes' for its 'colouring' but not for its 'character' or 'sentiment'), the poem does contain in miniature the 'knowledge of contrast, feeling for light and shade' that he stipulated as essentials for poetry. Whether the ending is meant to be spiritually uplifting or deflatingly down-to-earth (another draft of it by Keats seems to favour the latter reading) does not detract from the poem's over-all mood of youthful health and optimism. It was the last time that such an ambience was to appear untainted in Keats's work.

2.2.5 'La Belle Dame sans Merci'

Summary
In the season of late autumn an unidentified speaker questions the main character, a demobilised 'knight-at-arms', about the causes of his despondent attitude and unkempt appearance. In reply the knight describes the chance encounter that wrought this change in him. He has met a lady so beautiful as to seem scarcely human, 'a faery's

child', and has spent a day in her company, weaving adornments for her from nature's materials and receiving in return food and drink of strange and supernatural origin ('honey wild, and manna-dew'). The lady sings and speaks to him 'in language strange', and takes him to her underground home where, becoming saddened, she lulls him 'asleep'. While sleeping the knight dreams that he sees a heap of 'pale kings and princes', stacked like bones in a burial chamber, their mouths gaping wide in grotesque and 'horrid warning' against their enchanter and destroyer, the lady who knows no pity. At this point the knight awakes, devoid of company and barren of hope; and he wanders ever after through the desolate landscape that mirrors his own inner despair.

Commentary
The poem was written in April 1819, just prior to the major odes. It lacks the dialectic energy of the odes – their self-debating restiveness – but follows what seems to be a dream logic of its own. The poem's kinship with ballads – its abbreviated story-line, simplicity of diction and mingling of natural with supernatural characters – seems to place it among the roots of folk memory, so that the semiconscious quality of its distilled wisdom will be accorded greater tolerance, a 'willing suspension of disbelief' (in Coleridge's words), by its readers. The short emphatic line that punctuates the end of each stanza augments the poem's air of inevitability ('And nó bírds síng') by substituting assertion for explanation: this is so because it has always been so, and no other cause need be sought. The poem's fluid use of tenses, drifting between past and present (the sedge 'has withered' in stanza 1, but 'is withered' in stanza 12), reinforces its timeless atmosphere, its unfolding of an experience common to all men, not unique to one alone.

The nature of that experience remains enigmatic and is only half-articulated in the poem, probably because its intangibility is its very essence: it is a glimpse of the eternal world of perfect forms that is momentarily vouchsafed to the knight while on earth, a preview of paradise or what Keats called 'a shadow of reality to come' (letter to Bailey, 22 November 1817). Such beauty as the knight is privileged to behold for a while will, like the rainbow, evaporate the closer he tries to approach it, because its reality is spiritual not physical, eternal not mortal. It is a beauty that can only be beheld 'sidelong', not face to face, a beauty that is epitomised in Keat's dying recollection of Fanny Brawne: 'I eternally see her figure eternally vanishing' (letter to Brown, 30 September 1820).

The lady's exact significance and the reason for the knight's failure to remain with her are deliberately left dark, perhaps to invite the reader's imaginative projection of his own deepest longings upon the sparse landmarks of the narrative, tipping its 'few points . . . with the fine web of his soul' to 'weave a tapestry empyrean', as, Keats believed, 'almost any man' could do, with proper persuasion (letter to Reynolds, 19 February 1818). The poem's crypticness is part of its technique: each reader will fill in its gaps from his own emotional or intellectual reservoir.

A sonnet ('A Dream, after reading Dante's Episode of Paola and Francesca') written at about the same time and copied into Fanny Brawne's copy of Dante suggests that 'La Belle Dame' found at least part of its stimulus in Fanny, and in Keats's growing conviction that love and death were the same goal (see the end of 'Bright star'). In this sonnet the speaker beholds in a dream a face and a form that blend beauty and death inextricably, as if love opened the door to both life and death at once: 'Pale were the sweet lips I saw,/Pale were the lips I kissed'. The knight in 'La Belle Dame' similarly discovers love and death simultaneously, as the cries of his 'death-pale' fellow victims make clear.

The poem might also signify Keats's pursuit of the poetic muse as the source of all truth and beauty. Keats elsewhere uses horses to suggest the metric vehicle that carries the poem: 'Pegasus' and 'rocking horse', for instance, are metaphors for sublime and plodding metres respectively in 'Sleep and Poetry'. Thus the would-be poet in 'La Belle Dame' 'sets' his lady on his 'pacing steed', and is able for a time to harness his imagination and to proceed smoothly in the company of his vision. Eventually, however, the vision fades (as in 'Ode to a Nightingale') and the poet finds himself 'alone', bereft of even his metrical gifts, horseless and aimless, 'loitering' in the wilderness of his wasted dreams.

Whether the question is one of permanent partnership with unearthly beauty or of sustained transport on the wings of imagination, it is equally impossible of achievement. But the mere intimation of it awakens the knight to torture. The 'cold hill's side' is much colder and emptier after the dream than it was while he remained ignorant that such communion might be possible in (or out of) the world. His hope of transcendent state of being, suffused with love – carried there by Fanny or by poetry itself – is, in Matthew Arnold's words, 'as soon as kindled, cooled', leaving him 'palely loitering' without health or rest, infecting with his blighted vision the natural world which he still bodily, though not mentally, inhabits. He has been trapped by a vision of happiness unattainable on this earth; and the realisation of its unrealisability is what condemns him to this desultory existence. The mistake is in even hoping that such a state of perfect bliss could be reached in the material world – in confusing the 'elfin grot' where such things might occur, the supernatural sphere, with the 'gloam' of the limited light-and-shadow natural arena. Only death, towards which the protagonist seems irredeemably heading, may resolve the conundrum, either through apprehension of what is sought or through utter oblivion.

2.2.6 'Lamia'

Summary
Lamia is a hybrid creature with a serpent's body and a woman's face, an ambivalent being whose essence seems both supernatural and natural. Her share in the supernatural enables her to inform the god Hermes of the whereabouts of the nymph he is pursuing. Her earthly heritage is evident in her having fallen in love with a mortal, Lycius, 'a youth of Corinth'. In return for her assistance Hermes touches Lamia with his 'Caducean' wand and returns her to a 'woman's shape'. Lamia betakes herself to a wood near Corinth where she waylays Lycius, homeward-bound from a fishing trip. Overcome by her blandishments and her beauty, Lycius begs her to be his companion, even though he at first takes her for a goddess, someone beyond his reach. Lamia's eloquent exposition of 'woman's lore' convinces Lycius that she is 'a real woman' after all, and he goes off with her to the city. The passing shadow of Apollonius, Lycius's tutor 'robed in philosophic gown', warns Lamia that the fantasy web she is weaving around the ensnared Lycius may not hold for ever.

After some time spent in the seclusion of Lamia's stately residence, Lycius's consciousness is recalled to the external world by the sound of distant trumpets. A latent claustrophobia creeps up on him and, 'cruel grown', he demands that Lamia marry him publicly and give a feast at which he might show her off as his 'prize' to his acquaintances. Lamia reluctantly submits to his request and, with foreboding, summons the 'viewless servants' of her supernatural realm to prepare the banqueting hall for her earthly nuptials. The guests arrive, among them the uninvited Apollonius. At the height of the celebration Apollonius fixes his eyes on the 'alarmed beauty of the bride', staring at her icily until she withers beneath his gaze, finally vanishing 'with a frightful scream'. Traumatised by the sudden dissolution of all his dreams, Lycius dies the same night, his 'marriage robe' becoming his shroud.

Commentary
The poem was written between June and September 1819, during Keats's self-imposed exile from Fanny Brawne. It returns to the couplet form of *Endymion*, but the structure is tighter now, the syntax terser, the lines pruned of verbal excess. There is greater economy of style, so that the story proceeds relentlessly towards its foreshadowed conclusion at a gathering pace. Keats was sure that the poem exhibited more maturity than his earlier narratives, and that its heroine, a 'lovely graduate' of 'Cupid's college' (I, 197–8) and therefore sexually experienced, could not be accused of naïvety or arrested adolescence. 'I am certain there is that sort of fire in it which must take hold of people', he wrote confidently to his brother.

Yet 'Lamia' has succeeded in bemusing many readers, mainly because of the uncertain quality of its eponymous heroine. She is initially presented as a serpent, a reminder of the devouring power of love that does not escape the notice of Apollonius. The passion that galvanises Lamia promises to have ill effects: the grass, at her transformation from snake to woman, 'withered at dew so sweet and virulent' (I, 149). Her imprisonment in the 'wreathèd tomb' of the serpent's body indicates her kinship with Satan, the 'demon's self' (I, 38, 56), and her charms are described as 'Circean' (I, 115), hence threatening to degrade her admirers. Like Satan, she is unable to seduce her victim without his willing consent. These are the serpentine aspects of Lamia's constitution, the venomous elements that threaten to poison and destroy. But mixed with them is a curious, eventually overriding sense of Lamia's vulnerability, as if she really were 'a woman, and without/Any more subtle fluid in her veins/Than throbbing blood' (I, 306–8). This impression is aided by Lamia's association with images of fragility ('There she stood/About a young bird's flutter from a wood': I, 179–80) and by indications that she shares the same anxieties and uncertainties – the same dependence upon the beloved object – as her human partner, Lycius ('the self-same pains/Inhabited her frail-strung heart as his': I, 308–9).

The deadly hostility between Apollonius and Lamia also indicates some ambivalence in Keats's attitude. It suggests an incompatible animosity between intellect and emotion, neither of which is sufficient for a full life, since the former is 'cold' and implicitly sterile while the latter offers only a paradise for fools, an empty illusion. In 'Ode to Psyche', composed shortly before, Keats had managed to wed intellect and feeling: now they seem to occupy different dimensions, as Lamia's palace is invisible to the men in the street who do not share Lycius's trust in imaginative fantasy ('the most curious/Were foiled, who watched to trace them to their house': I, 392–3). Lycius seems to be offered a choice that is mutually exclusive: to inhabit the poetic world of art and love, in both of which practices Lamia is adept, or to dwell in the austere but 'real' world of rational philosophy.

At this time in his life Keats was debating with himself the value of poetry, which often seemed 'in itself a nothing'. Philosophy, on the other hand, seemed more productive of general social good. In the middle of composing 'Lamia' Keats wrote to Reynolds, 'I am convinced more and more day by day that fine writing is, next to fine doing, the top thing in the world' (24 August 1819). Poetry was just a step towards something higher, a narcissistically self-indulgent enterprise when compared with the active philanthropy of 'fine doing'. Thus Apollonius the rationalist has Keats's intellectual approval, but his emotional sympathies are with Lamia, the fabricator of dream worlds out of airy nothings. For all her supernatural connections,

Lamia is powerless to prevent her human opponent from reducing her magical domain to mere rubble, 'empty of delight' (II, 307). Lycius's subsequent death suggests that even if love with its attendant solace is only a mirage, to puncture someone's fantasy is a cruelty akin to murder. Philosophy may have reason on its side, but it proves its point by devastating the soul that puts its trust in beauty. It has shrunk the universe down to a 'dull catalogue of common things' (II, 232) where angels and rainbows are duly defined and pigeonholed in alphabetical order. Apollonius's analytical eye may penetrate to the corrupt core of the fabric woven by Lamia for Lycius's pleasure, but he has nothing to put in place of what he has destroyed.

The poem has much beauty. There is rich visual description in Lamia's metamorphosis, where brilliant colours and astronomical bodies convulse together to suggest a rebirth that is also a cosmic upheaval (I, 146–66). Intense emotion is expressed in pithy lucid images (Lycius looks in Lamia's 'open eyes/Where he was mirrored small in paradise': II, 46–7). The Alexandrine is deftly deployed to stretch the pentameter (a line of five feet) and give to its meaning a sense of sinuousness ('the Nereids fair/Wind into Thetis' bower by many a pearly stair': I, 207–8) or elongation ('There ran a stream of lamps straight on from wall to wall': II, 131). Moments of crisis are conveyed in images that condense much of the thematic development, so that when, for example, Lycius first becomes aware of Lamia's paralysis, 'The myrtle sickened in a thousand wreaths' (II, 264), indicating that what was healthy, even natural, while he believed in it, decays and withers the instant that doubt creeps in.

Lamia and Lycius are both self-deceivers. Lamia makes the fatal mistake – which Lycius goes along with – of offering pleasure unalloyed by pain. She is able 'To unperplex bliss from its neighbour pain,/ . . . and estrange/Their points of contact' (I, 192–4). The raving 'mistress' of 'Ode on Melancholy' offers more durable rewards because the joy she brings is compounded with sorrow; and Lycius experiences a similarly mixed emotion when, on his first encounter with Lamia, he 'Swooned, murmuring of love, and pale with pain' (I, 289). When the pain subsequently disappears from the relationship, Lycius's suspicions ought to be aroused, and he seems aware that the exclusion of pain – and of the sort of scepticism that Apollonius would advocate – is somehow wrong, for he guiltily attempts to avoid contact with any of his former acquaintances: 'Muffling his face, of greeting friends in fear' (I, 362). Lamia's palace becomes a mock-cathedral (with 'mimic' trees in the 'aislèd place' instead of Gothic columns) for a secular and sensuous wedding, as if the concentration on hedonistic delights to the exclusion of pain or discomfort prevented Lycius from developing spiritually, thus rendering his love (and life) extremely brittle. Lycius's reckless embrace of the pleasure that offers itself and his readiness to believe wholeheartedly in the possibility of a life without sorrow or imperfection leads him literally to a dead end. It is a poem in which everybody's vision is impaired, everyone's philosophy inadequate, a situation which Keats set out to remedy in 'The Fall of Hyperion'.

2.2.7 'The Fall of Hyperion'

Summary
Canto I begins by discriminating between the dreams of 'Fanatics' and those of 'Poets', favouring the latter because they can be captured in the imprint of writing. The speaker, leaving unresolved the question of whether he is poet or mere fanatic, recounts a dream in which he stood in a flower-filled garden amid the aftermath of a feast. Quenching his thirst from a 'vessel' among the leftovers, he falls into a 'cloudy swoon' and has a further vision, a dream within a dream. He finds himself in a huge temple in which the accoutrements of several religions are lying about in an abandoned manner. His gaze focuses on an immense 'Image, huge of feature as a cloud', at whose altar a priestess is burning incense. From behind the 'fragrant curtains' of this smoking offering he hears a voice proclaim his demise if he does not immediately climb the steps to the altar. Endeavouring to do so, the speaker is struck by paralysis and feels the icy clutch of death around his heart. With immense effort he struggles to the bottom step and is at once carried up into the presence of the priestess, Moneta, a 'veilèd shadow'. She pours scorn on his poetic pretensions, categorising him as a mere self-pleasing 'dreamer' rather than a true poet who benefits others by his arduous toil.

Having vented her spleen on him, Moneta (later referred to as 'Mnemosyne' or 'memory') relents to the extent of offering to disclose to him the story of Saturn's defeat at the hands of Apollo, her 'foster child'. The speaker is then transported to a third level of dream, where he finds himself being guided by Moneta through the shrouded vale where Saturn is sitting, as motionless as his 'Image' in the temple. Thea approaches and tries to stir Saturn from his reverie. Failing in this, she falls 'weeping at his feet', a posture she maintains for an entire month, to the physical discomfort and eventually suicidal despair of the watching speaker. At length Saturn looks around him, making the acid observation that nature is thriving as usual while he and his erstwhile 'influence benign' have become superfluous. His harangue peters out in peevish self-pity, in 'poor and sickly sounding phrase'.

In Canto II Moneta explains that she is translating spiritual events into a language fit for mortal ear, 'humanizing' her account so that the speaker might grasp it. In this language of diminished grandeur she goes on to introduce the sun-god Hyperion, pacing through his palace with the nervous anger of a tenant unexpectedly given notice to quit. As he 'flares' on through his insecure domain, the poem breaks off.

Commentary

Dissatisfied with the earlier 'Hyperion', Keats attempted, in the summer of 1819, to remodel the poem by introducing a human figure among the supernatural personnel, in an effort to relate more closely the significance of events in the cosmic arena to human life. The first 293 lines of Canto I present the new frame for the story, but they also contain a digressionary debate, between Moneta and the speaker, on the function of the poet: a debate so probing and open-ended that the resumption of the narrative of Saturn's dethronement (repeated, with some modifications, from Book I of 'Hyperion') is an anticlimax, an irrelevance even. The poet who argues with Moneta, with such uncertainty and tenacity combined, is the new Keats; whereas the poet who reiterates the saga of the Titans' fall is the Keats of the previous year, a self he had in fact outgrown. It is more likely that this realisation, rather than his declared aversion to the 'Miltonic inversions' in the poem, was the reason why Keats finally laid the poem to rest in September 1819.

The architecture of the temple is Keats's attempt to realise in poetry the metaphor of life as 'a large mansion of many apartments', expounded in his letter to Reynolds (3 May 1818). Passing through this mansion, the thinking man is educated to an awareness of suffering. All the doors lead ultimately to 'dark passages' where moral certitudes are thrown into confusion: 'We see not the balance of good and evil. We are in a mist'. It is these dark passages that Moneta instructs the poet to traverse if he wishes to complete his apprenticeship. The source of poetic wisdom seems to lie in deep, possibly dangerous crevices of the mind, a terrain to which only the dreamer can gain access.

The 'fanatic' and the 'savage' may luxuriate in that state of indolence where impressions are received and associations made, the state of the 'dreamer'; but only the extraordinary energy of the poet can turn these impressions to good account, actively selecting and shaping them, giving to them a form which is apprehensible to others, rescuing them from oblivion: 'the fine spell of words alone can save/Imagination from the sable charm/And dumb enchantment' (I, 9–11). This is the difference between sleep and poetry, between source and artifact, between dreamer and poet.

The poet's first dream, of being in an Eden-like garden with vestiges of 'our Mother Eve' amid 'Palm, myrtle, oak, and sycamore, and beech' (I, 20–31) and other natural objects, incarnates the cluttered Elysian fields of the savage who 'guesses at Heaven'. But such a profusion of sensual delights operates as a barrier ('made a screen') to the naked and painful truths which the poet must confront. So he proceeds to a deeper dream-level and finds himself in a more spiritual state but in less material surroundings: 'I started up/As if with wings; but the fair trees were gone' (I, 58–9).

The chamber in which the poet now finds himself has a sacred atmosphere, 'an old sanctuary with roof august' (I, 62), which combines Christian solemnity ('grey cathedrals, buttressed walls') with pagan richness ('Robes, golden tongs, censer and chafing dish') in order to provide an appropriate setting for exploring what Keats elsewhere called 'the holiness of the heart's affections'. Christianity provides the spiritual sanction while Greece and Rome supply sensuous material items to indicate the interdependence of soul and body. The dominant impressions of this 'sanctuary' are of the unknown ('columns north and south, ending in mist/Of nothing': I, 84–5), of death ('black gates/Were shut against the sunrise evermore: I, 85–6) and disorientation (the altar of the 'Image' is in 'the west' rather than, more commonly, the east of the building). The poet has gone beyond the pleasure principle and beyond the realm of moral certainties to a cold and obscure source where life and death merge into the same cloudy essence. Moneta, 'the tall shade, in drooping linens veiled' (I, 216), resembles Milton's Death 'that shadow seemed' (*Paradise Lost*, II, 669), similarly vague in outline. The emptiness of the temple is striking: 'I sure should see/Other men here: but I am here alone' (I, 159–60). The quest that the poet has embarked on is a lonely one, involving severance from the rest of his kind, who, says Moneta, 'seek no wonder but the human face' (I, 163): they have no desire to penetrate the inner veils of experience and peer into the heart of darkness.

Comprehension of 'the miseries of the world' requires a chilling isolation from contact human or divine. Unaided by man or God, the poet risks being any moment overwhelmed by unforeseen forces. He must either perish or press onward and save himself. It is an ordeal that the poet almost fails; his struggle results ultimately in a success that implies his passing to a higher plane of consciousness ('I mounted up': I, 134). The height he has 'usurped' through sheer intensity of effort is a mental eminence, a 'fane' (I, 152), a temple in some 'region of [the] mind' ('Ode to Psyche'), whence the poet may see, feel and understand the manifold sufferings of his fellows. Out of this awareness comes insight and the poetry to 'medicine' his peers. Thus the pursuit of poetry is not 'ignoble', nor is the seclusion necessary to its creation ultimately selfish, since its end is beneficial to humanity. The poet is a 'humanist, physician to all men' (I, 183–90).

As yet the speaker of the poem is still in the 'dreamer' category, for despite the 'prodigious . . . toil' (I, 121) that has so far saved him from extinction, he has yet to cast off all his habits of self-gratification and reach the height of true austerity, absolute negative capability, complete mastery of suffering and comprehension of its heuristic value as a means of spiritual education.

Moneta is the archetype of death and is therefore eternally dying without ever attaining the final dissolution that individuals accomplish. She is 'deathwards progressing/To no death' (I, 260–1); the lifeless pallor of her skin is beyond comparison with conventional images of whiteness ('passed/The lily and the snow'). At the same time she is Mnemosyne, the mother of the muses and the progenitress of poetry. Thus her deathly paleness signifies that poetic effort is literally a sacrifice of the self. The speaker, too, undergoes the experience of dying ('the cold/Grew stifling, suffocating, at the heart': I, 129–30). Moneta's gaze is completely inward-looking. The poet must be similarly self-communing and self-consuming, and will then, unbeknown to himself, illuminate mankind even while burning himself out, glowing like the indifferent moon 'who knows not/What eyes are upward cast' (I, 270–1).

Saturn's image has undefined contours ('an Image huge'), suggesting a clumsy lack of refinement and a remoteness from humanity, and summarising what Keats calls the 'superannuations' (I, 68) of a belief-system that is no longer useful. Saturn's reign may be over but, as 'Hyperion' makes clear, that is only because it has been replaced by a new aesthetic creed in the natural course of history. It is not merely ended, but transcended. Saturn, unnaturally, wants to reverse the course of aesthetic, or spiritual, history: 'Throw down those imps, and give me victory' (I, 431). But this defiance is querulous and 'feeble'. What should, judging by its appearance, be a god (Saturn's 'Image . . . whose face I cannot see': I, 213) speaks merely like 'some old man of the earth' (I, 440). There is no 'unison' between the 'large-limbed visions' of the gods and their ill-tempered utterances: where the poet expects to hear the 'dolorous accent from a tragic harp', he hears only 'poor and sickly sounding' (I, 439–44).

Where the new version of 'Hyperion' develops out of the old is in this area of religious 'superannuation', the pensioning-off of the old gods, including the Christian deity. The apotheosis of the new god Apollo, so crucial to the earlier poem, has become irrelevant to the concerns of the later one. The consequence is that the poet now drifts free of all moorings, ready to explore experience without any traditional guidelines. He turns towards the void, casts caution and his old self to the winds and prepares to face the mystery of life – a mystery that remains opaque and irreducible despite his effort to penetrate it. Refusing to simplify or take refuge in a pat answer or a uniform set of symbols, the speaker embarks intrepidly on a lone night-journey without landmarks. The unillusioned honesty of Keats's last, unfinished narrative poem (aside from the unpolished satirical fragment, 'The Cap and Bells'), and the spare monotone in which it is delivered, reveal how far he had come in the space of two years, from the cloying 'sweets' of *Endymion*.

44

2.3 ODES

2.3.1 'Ode to Psyche'

Summary

Psyche, goddess of the mind or soul, was a latecomer to the Greek pantheon and was never worshipped with the degree of fervour that earlier deities basked in. The poet states his intention of redressing the balance: he will be her 'choir' and his ode the hymn to compensate for her lack of adoration in classical times. The poet is inspired to do this after beholding Psyche and Cupid ('love') in a dream, recumbent in a post-coital posture amid a sylvan setting. He wishes to commemorate the union of intellect and emotion, to pay homage to the presence of the spiritual in the physical world, even though present times are not propitious to such a celebration.

Commentary

The poem was written towards the end of April 1819 and was the first of Keats's major odes. The ode structure allows a more expanded treatment of the subject than is possible in sonnets, while still encouraging a compressed statement. The ode is an appropriate form for thinking aloud, for holding a discussion with oneself on a defined topic. It is ideal for unfolding an argument of limited duration. Each stanza becomes a chunk of thought, a dialectical step, sometimes contradicting the previous argumentative 'block', sometimes complementing it. Lines and stanzas can be dilated or contracted to accommodate the contours of the argument as it develops. Keats was learning about the technical flexibility of the form through writing 'Ode to Psyche', and he put his lessons to good effect in the subsequent odes with their meatier subject matter and pithier phrasing.

The legend told of Psyche's murder by Venus as punishment for attracting the love of the latter's son Cupid. Cupid applies to Jupiter for Psyche's immortalisation, a plea that is granted. In the course of the affair Psyche has suffered estrangement from her lover and endures an exile of wandering before finding happiness again in Cupid's arms. It is this aspect of the legend that most interested Keats, because it seemed an allegory of his own idea, expounded shortly before in his letter to George, about the soul being schooled through suffering. There he suggested that, although the human race may compromise 'millions' of 'intelligences', which are 'atoms of perception' or 'sparks of divinity', these 'intelligences' are not 'souls till they acquire identities'; and this they can only do through suffering, which is 'a system of spirit-creation'. The soul is thus educated into an awarenes of itself ('identity') through suffering. Individual suffering, felt 'on the pulses', offers lessons superior to those supplied by Christianity ('I think it a grander system of salvation than the Christian religion'). Keats may have seen Psyche's term of painful and loveless wandering as a parallel to the situation of the lonely poet, alienated from his fellow men for a time, doomed to suffer physically and mentally until his spiritual formation is complete and he can see with the heightened awareness of an immortal being (though dreaming, the poet sees Psyche 'with awakened eyes', his consciousness having expanded through sympathy with her sufferings).

Having passed through the 'vale of soul-making', Psyche now partakes of divine essence – she is 'wingèd' – but she retains her humanity, too. The stress on the physical basis of her relationship with Cupid suggests that love, as well as poetry, is another means of 'self-destroying' (*Endymion*, I, 799) by which the individual can shed his limiting ego-bound selfish shell and assume a more cosmic and generous 'identity':

> Their arms embraced, and their pinions too;
> Their lips touched not, but had not bade adieu.

This is a consummation both physical and spiritual, both human and divine, but the emphasis on the natural setting ('In deepest grass, beneath the whispering roof/Of leaves and tremblèd blossoms') suggests that Keats is depicting a human, not an angelic condition: the state of the soul ('Psyche') once it has undergone all the trials of this world. It is then simultaneously both above the world ('wingèd') and on it ('in a forest'), inseparable from the suffering body through which it has gained its promotion.

Psyche has no 'temple', 'shrine' or 'oracle', because the idea she represents to Keats is a more sophisticated one than any posited by the old religions. Even the most recent generation of gods, according to the genealogy of 'Hyperion', has become obsolete ('Olympus' faded hierarchy'). The idea of transcendence of the bodily prison-house through suffering needs no concrete edifice to establish it and pin it down. It is an imaginative theology and hence its properties are constructed more appropriately in mental than in physical space, which is what Keats proceeds to do ('I will . . . build a fane/In some untrodden region of my mind'). In contrast to earlier times when nature itself seemed to provide the location for the elemental gods ('When holy were the haunted forest boughs,/Holy the air, the water, and the fire'), these gods may now be internalised and find their abodes in the brain of the poet, who moreover is no longer the entranced semi-conscious mouthpiece of subliminal forces ('no heat/ Of pale-mouthed prophet dreaming') but the hyperconscious seer ('by my own eyes inspired') able to marshal his perceptions into a new unfaded hierarchy.

Psyche is located not in external nature, where 'pines . . . murmur in the wind', but in the recesses of the brain, aided by its faculty of imagination ('the gardener Fancy . . ./Who breeding flowers, will never breed the same'), which continually recreates experience in unexpected ways. Ultimately the poet, Psyche, imagination and love are all fused together, the light from the 'bright torch' illuminating a new, fully-integrated being. The belief in the godlike power given to man when love and psyche coalesce in him to lift him from his earthly frame is evident in some lines from *Otho the Great*, the abortive drama that Keats was working on in the summer of 1819:

> at the kiss
> Of Psyche given by Love, there was a buzz
> Among the gods!
>
> (V, v, 28–30)

'Ode to Psyche' gave Keats useful technical training in the form that was to be the vehicle for his most distilled and mature meditations. As an apprentice work, though, it has some defects. The poem displays a diffuseness and repetitiveness, despite Keats's claim in his letter to George that it was 'the only one with which I have taken even moderate pains'. There is also a lack of tension, no tugging to and fro between different strains of argument, since the struggle between time and eternity, flesh and spirit, physics and metaphysics, has already been resolved in the union of Psyche and Love before the poem has begun. By the time the poet meets them in the first stanza the consummation is already accomplished ('They lay calm-breathing on the bedded grass') and placidity, even complacency, reigns. The temptation to escapism against which Keats had been stalwartly fighting since throwing off Leigh Hunt's influence seems to be creeping in again in the lush garden of 'hushed, cool-rooted flowers, fragrant-eyed' from which serpents and other ill omens have been excluded.

The poem's promise, however, is fulfilled in the ensuing poems, narratives as well as odes. Keats bravely explored the 'untrodden region' of his mind in 'The Fall of Hyperion' and he tried to 'win' a consolatory truth for his readers from his wrestling matches with 'shadowy thought' in his other odes. 'Ode to Psyche' maps out the territory that Keats was shortly to investigate within the 'wreathed trellis', the undiscovered network, of his 'working brain'.

2.3.2 'Ode on a Grecian Urn'

Summary
Through studying the motifs embossed on an ancient Greek funeral vase, the poet is aroused into a contemplation of the perplexing

ironies of human life. The figures on the vase, though cold and bloodless, have achieved a perfection in their immobility that is denied their more volatile flesh-and-blood counterparts. Art has moulded a completeness, an eternity that life can only sigh for. The characters whose story is pictured on the urn are all engaged in some uncompleted activity: the flautist is frozen by the sculptor's hand in the midst of his musical air, the lovers are closing for a never-to-be-consummated kiss, the priest prepares an animal for a ritual slaughter that is indefinitely postponed and the townspeople will sport their mood of festive gaiety to the end of time. The anticlimax, the satiety that sets in upon completion of all human endeavour is unknown to the beings in the sculpted world of the urn. Though none of them has attained the object of his or her desire, each lives in a state of candid hope and expectation that time and experience will never disappoint. Their ignorance is bliss when compared with the poet's worldly wisdom.

The art that the urn embodies tantalises the poet, and all who scrutinise it, with the possibility of a world forever green, where emotion is always innocent and the mind pellucidly clear. Such a place of perennial spring, unravaged by time or disease and un-touched by corporal baseness, exists as an idealised topography – a foreglimpse of paradise – created and refined by art. By means of an assurance addressed directly to the imagination, the 'text' of the urn's story will continue to provide succour and sustenance to whoever reads it.

Commentary

Written in the late spring of 1819, shortly after 'Ode to Psyche', this ode exemplifies the complexity of the mature Keats's response to life, and his refusal to seek refuge in an easy or indolent solution. Although some critics have denounced the last two lines as being too simplistic or banal, the urn's final gnomic utterance provides the only possible termination to the oppositions that have unwound in the previous stanzas. Keats develops these oppositions by demonstrating that neither the world of life nor the realm of art is perfect. The lover in the real world may feel sated or sickened once he has achieved his goal, but the lover within the frame of art must rest perpetually unsatisfied. Despite the attractions of an endless springtime, the trees on the vase are petrified in unnatural stiffness and the shepherd's pipe hangs poised in mute futility. It is a cold and silent pastoral scene, and its adjacent town has the air of a place rendered desolate, empty, unpeopled as if by a plague.

There is an equivocalness in the poet's attitude to the classical world of the Grecian urn, despite his proclaimed preference for it over the imperfect world in which he draws breath. This ambiguity feeds the basic tension between the two worlds of life and art in the poem: an opposition which can only be resolved, if at all, by the ultimate declamation of the equality between beauty and truth.

Ambiguity is introduced in the first line of the ode. Is 'still' an adverb (meaning 'yet'), or an adjective (meaning 'motionless')? The unspeaking vase, wedded to quietness, remains virginal, unviolated: it retains its mystery. The urn does not speak plainly; in fact, it tempts its scrutiniser into doing the talking, in formulating his response to it. It provokes him to ponder, while it remains enigmatically silent, 'still unravished', declining to dictate the answers to the gaps in the observer's understanding, but encouraging him to stretch his intellectual resources to cover them.

The poet, addressing himself to the urn, thinks of it as an orphaned production, having its first cause in its creator but depending on history to shape its character. Owing to the passage of time the observer now reads a very different story in the vase from that which its shaper first intended. What must once have been self-evident to those who viewed it – the divine or human quality of its personages – has since evolved into a subject of speculation: 'What men or gods are these?' For all of its uncertainty, or perhaps because of it, the static art of classical sculpture can convey a 'tale more sweetly' than the kinetic arts of poetry and music, possibly because the latter can only unfold their being through measures of time. Sculpture's monumental immobility expresses a contemptuous disregard for the passage of time. Its wordless communication is more effective than the poet's clumsy efforts to convey deep truths in unwieldy language. But notwithstanding Keats's promotion of sculpture above his own sphere of poetry, he is using the latter to fill out the hollowness of the embroidered vase. His ode, with its subtle shifts of rhythm and its interwoven rhymes to match alteration or congruence of thought, is itself a reproduction and embellishment of the urn in another medium; and his gallant disclaimer of poetic merit is not to be taken at face value, but contributes to the complexity of attitude that the poem exhibits.

A prime tenet of that attitude is that things implicit are more captivating or compelling than things explicit: the unheard song is sweeter than the tune fully rounded out for the ear's absorption. Expectation is better than repletion: the dream nourishes, the reality palls. In stanzas 2 and 3 the music that plays on the surface of the silent urn is supplied according to the fancy of the beholder: any realised melody would be flawed in comparison with the perfect one constructed in the inner ear of imagination. Similarly the promise of love is greater than its fulfilment: the deficiencies intrinsic to the actual experience are discounted so long as hope springs eternal. The poet makes a point of contrasting his own jaded appetite, as one who has tasted the fruit of love and found it bitter, with the sweet sensations of those who have yet to make the discovery. It may be that this is a ploy to draw attention obliquely to his own disconsolate situation, his 'lover's case' (in Sir Philip Sidney's phrase): his 'burning forehead' and 'parching tongue'. In other words, his rumination on the subject of the vase, like his meditation on the song of the nightingale in the subsequent ode, recoils and comes to rest on the solitary self of the speaker. And the feverish manifestations that erupt in the last line of stanza 3 may not simply be signs of the sickness endemic in physical love but could be symptomatic of the tubercular illness that was soon to destroy Keats. Here the poem has left the patterned world of Arcadia and gazes into a void; and for a brief moment it teeters on the brink of becoming a different poem altogether.

In stanza 4, however, equilibrium is recovered. The poet anchors his attention once more on the consolingly placid and reassuringly unchanging world of the urn. Once his imagination has material to feed upon and his curiosity is stimulated to continue its questioning, mental health is restored, although the meditation now assumes a darker tone. What he sees depicted on the urn now prompts him to probe into what has *not* been portrayed there. The little town, with its silent streets to which no inhabitant will ever return, is conjured up as vividly in the poem as the scenes 'copied' from the urn. It gives the impression that time has after all effected tremendous changes in the sculpted world, which can no more avoid the apocalypse than can the 'natural' world.

So the ostensible argument in favour of art's supremacy is weighted with ambivalence. There is surely sterility in a fruitless quest, in a goal that can 'never, never' be reached. In the inferior world of human passion there is at least experience, and even the 'heart high-sorrowful' can, in the light of Keats's ideas on the 'vale of soul-making', learn a lesson and forge for itself an identity denied to those whose being has been perfected by the artist's touch. The other side of the artistic vision, like the 'desolate' town on the other side of the urn, is emptiness, a human void. Art needs the materials of life, its chaos and asymmetry, if it is not to atrophy into 'cold' marble, an ornament without human application.

By the end of the poem Keats is beginning to merge his two worlds – the apparently perfect and timeless world of art and the innately corrupt and mutable world of the flesh – and to imply that inadequacy and unfulfilment are to be found in each. As in 'Ode to a Nightingale', the original flight of fancy cannot be sustained indefinitely but must sooner or later fall back to earth. Hence there is no logical conclusion at which the ode can arrive; there is no simple choice between 'art' and 'life', since each bears the seeds of its imperfection. All that the poet can deduce is that the urn stimulates, gratifies and consoles him, he knows not why.

The urn keeps its secret intact, having successfully 'teased us out of thought'. Its final message is formed from the interaction between it and its interpreter. Since it is still the 'foster-child of silence', the 'say'st' that precedes its message has a metaphorical not a literal inference. The urn still says nothing; its absolute beauty puts words into the mouth of the beholder, words which themselves constitute an endlessly circular argument, 'Beauty is truth, truth beauty', of more incantatory than semantic value. The beauty, itself unanalysable, of the poem 'teases us' to the ultimate conclusion that whatever solace the probings of the artistic mind may have to offer to the human spirit can be sensed but not systematised. Thus the 'eternity' of art has another relevance. Art is eternal because the truths it 'intimates'(in Wordsworth's expression) remain forever tantalisingly just beyond the grasp of man's rational apprehension, and hence of his ability to capture and preserve them in the amber of language.

The theme of the whole poem and its crystallisation in the last two lines may be summarised as follows. Truth cannot be reached by reasoning processes or logical steps (whereas 'fact' can), but only by a leap of the imagination, which can hold all the anomalies of experience together for a fragile moment, as iridescence is imprisoned in a bubble.

2.3.3 'Ode to a Nightingale'

Summary
The speaker confesses to feeling depressed and lethargic, as if his senses had been deadened by a drug. The singing nightingale has provoked this despondency, not because the speaker envies the bird but because his sympathetic participation in the joy of its song has, paradoxically, been so extreme ('being too happy in thine happiness') as to incite a contrary emotion. The antidote to his depression, he assumes at first, must be something which will empower him to forget the weight of his human body and soar with the bird to an imagined worlds ('some melodious plot') where fancy can become reality. The properties of wine are considered, its propensity for throwing a pall of benign oblivion over the tormented mind is applauded, but an alcoholic solution is eventually rejected as too escapist, perhaps too temporary. A more permanent remedy might be found in poetry; and no sooner does the speaker incline this way than his intuition is rewarded. Poetry allows him to join the nightingale with his intellect intact, which is preferable to the insensate torpor ('the forest dim') that alcohol might induce.

His delighted astonishment at being able to fly to the nightingale unimpeded, through the faculty of his imagination, endures a brief moment before he realises that his goal has been but half achieved. He beholds the 'Queen-Moon' and her 'starry' subordinates with his mind's eye, illuminating them with poetical fire, but his physical eye remains 'darkling' in his physical body, unable to 'see' the nightingale's habitat and reduced to 'guessing' its vegetation by snuffing its odours. The speaker's ability to merge with the bird and lose his painful self-identity is thus qualified. Nevertheless, listening in separation to the bird's ebullient performance, he is tempted with the thought that, in the words of Shakespeare's Othello, 'If it were now to die, /'Twere now to be most happy' (*Othello*, II, i, 187–8).

The nascent death-wish, however, is quickly stifled when the speaker reflects that death might after all impose utter insensibility, the extinction of all his faculties, and he would no longer be able to hear the bird's other-worldly emissions ('To thy high requiem become a sod'). Unlike himself, the nightingale seems eternal. Its song floats ethereal and unchanged through all the aeons of history; the same melody that the speaker listens to today has been heard by rich and poor alike since the dawn of consciousness, in locations secular and biblical, and even in supernatural regions untrodden by the foot of man ('forlorn'). This last speculation serves to remind the speaker of his own isolation, of the unbridgeable gap between the bright immortal world glimpsed through the nightingale's song and the pale mortal sphere in which he is condemned to fulfil his destiny. His imagination ('the fancy') has enabled him to suspend reality for a while and unite his soul with the nightingale's song, but such a respite from the world of painful experience cannot continue indefinitely. Finally, not only the illusion of transcendence but the sound of the song itself evaporates, and the speaker is left wondering whether he has been privileged with an 'intimation of immortality' (in Wordsworth's words) or whether he has simply been the victim of an inconsequential day-dream.

Commentary

The poem was written at the same time as 'Ode on a Grecian Urn', in late spring 1819. Some critics claim that it was the earlier of the two, partly because the 'Urn's' air of affirmation, especially at the end, seems closer to 'Autumn's' calm attitude of acceptance, whereas 'Nightingale' is more hesitant in its approach and ends irresolutely asking questions instead of marshalling declarative epigrams. It might on the other hand be argued that the poem's heightened dialectic, its more extreme alternation between positive and negative moods leading to a less assured finale, is an advance on the rotund assurances that reverberate from the Grecian urn. Keats, in other words, has entered that 'mist' mentioned in his 'mansion of many apartments' letter, the cloud of unknowing that was to absorb him in his last, incomplete poem 'The Fall of Hyperion'.

Whichever ode was written first, the same preoccupation with the inadequacies of human life and the possibility of an alternative world beyond the confines of space and time predominates. In 'Urn' it is the realm of art that offers the escape, in 'Nightingale' it is the voice of nature. The overtures from both worlds are responded to in the respective odes, their topographies are explored and their limitations exposed.

In this poem the speaker, catching the nightingale's song and surprised by the sound of such beauty in a world of dissolution and ugliness, 'where men sit and hear each other groan', seeks to pursue it to an idealised mental paradise where perpetual springtime ('mid-May') reigns, bathing in light 'from heaven'. This is an imaginative leap ('Already with thee!') rather than a labour of logic ('the dull brain perplexes and retards'), but one that cannot remain airborne for ever. As the ode unfolds inexorably according to strict measures of time and space, following the metrical pattern of its stanzas (ten iambic lines rhyming *ababcdecde*, all pentameter except for the shorter eighth line, a trimeter of three feet), so the 'forlorn' poet must eventually relinquish his fancied proximity to the nightingale, replant his feet on trodden earth and hearken passively while the music of the bird, the ecstatic language of another, mythical frame of existence, fades gradually away from the terrestrial scene ('Past the near meadows, over the still stream,/Up the hill-side') back into the eternal spiritual world where Ruth still stands in tears amid the alien corn.

Unlike the language of men, the nightingale's song does not evolve: it is unaffected by the passage of time, but remains the same as it always was, which seems to render it a trustworthy key to open the door or the 'magic casement' into that eternal world which the speaker is yearning to enter. Another key to it could be that of death. Though there is no guarantee that ceasing upon the midnight with no pain will admit the suffering human soul to an existence commensurate with its capacity for enjoyment ('we shall enjoy ourselves hereafter by having what we called happiness on earth repeated in a finer tone and so repeated', wrote Keats to Bailey on 22 November 1817), there seems to be a certainty, absent from 'Urn', that continuation in life promises nothing but suffering and exhaustion, to no profitable end unless it be to create such imagined worlds as 'Ode to a Nightingale' as a refuge for the sorely tried spirit to fly to momentarily.

The 'half-in-love' affair with death is ultimately quashed when the other 'half' presents itself to Keats's awareness at the close of the sixth stanza. Once dead he might simply be a 'sod', completely oblivious and incapable of receiving the nightingale's song or any impressions from worlds physical or metaphysical. The poem ends unresolved, concluding with an interrogation that must remain unanswered. The 'chameleon' poet ends up questioning everything, even whether his most palpable but now faded vision of the garden-paradise for ailing human souls ever occured to him at all ('Fled is that music'). The teasing anomalies of Keats's mature odes are expressed partly through such fluctuations of temperament, measuring the unsatisfactoriness of earthly life against the unknowability of an unearthly one, and never able to penetrate entirely through to a vision that could absorb and transcend them both.

As if to demonstrate its belief in the flawed quality of the human condition, the poem evinces some imperfection. Most noticeable is its failure to achieve the spiritual elevation through suffering implicit in the 'Grecian Urn's 'high-sorrowful' heart. In 'Nightingale' the suffering is merely a physical freight, an unalleviated and unprofitable dead weight: 'sorrow' invokes only 'leaden-eyed despairs'. Pain is spurned, not integrated, unusually for Keats's mature work. It could be said, on the other hand, that the ode in its entirety and the failure of its quest constitute a more comprehensive kind of educative 'sorrow'. The poem has also attracted criticism for its diction, which ranges from the medical realism of stanza 2 to quaint archaisms such as 'elf' in stanza 8. In its defence it might be argued that such extremes of style are indicative of the speaker's uncertain oscillation between the imagined land of his heart's desire and the world he knows where 'youth grows pale, and spectre-thin, and dies'. Besides, the word 'elf' is peculiarly appropriate as an image of the poet's vagrant fancy. If an elf is a being on the boundary between the natural and the supernatural, glimpsed by some but not by the sceptical, it seems an apt metaphor for the imagination which, throughout the poem, has been flitting about in the twilight zone between starry fays and the deep-delved earth.

In its honest appraisal of the insufficiency of humanity, incarcerated in its sensual world – a world both delectable and deplorable – yet unable to convince itself that beauty here points to beatitude hereafter, 'Ode to a Nightingale' addresses an anxiety that has haunted mankind since 'ancient days'. The couching of the terms of its internal debate in vivid and sparkling imagery 'winkins at the brink' of inexpressible insight has made this one of the most popular of all English poems.

2.3.4 'Ode on Melancholy'

Summary
The reader or listener is exhorted to turn away from the conventional symbols of death – the river of oblivion in hell, poisonous plants such as deadly nightshade, the yew trees that gather in graveyards, insects with the mark of death upon them and birds that act as its harbinger – at times of depression. For to brood thus over its insignia would be a perverse act of self-indulgence, resulting in the soul itself succumbing to the noxious influence of lethargy.

Instead the sufferer from melancholy should focus his attention on beautiful objects that normally kindle a pleasurable response in the spirit that greets them: delicate flowers, the iridescent spectrum of the natural world and especially the unfathomable depths in the eyes of a loved one. Such a forced mating of low spirits and elevated objects will not jolt the sufferer from this melancholic train of thought, but it will solace him in so far as it shows him the kinship between joy and sorrow, two emotions that are apparently contradictory but which in fact nourish each other.

Commentary

Written in May 1819, this ode is generally regarded as inferior to the three great odes that encompass it; mainly because it neither presents an unfolding dialectic in which the progress of the verse matches the process of the debate (as 'Urn' and 'Nightingale' do), medium and matter being inseparably interwoven, nor does it suggest a wholly matured, if static vision (as 'Autumn' does), sufficient unto itself. The conclusion of 'Ode on Melancholy' is already anticipated in its opening injunction ('No, no, go not to Lethe'). Although this warning springs from Keats's deeply-held conviction that pleasure and pain have an intimate and mutually fructifying relationship, this is not a conviction that is arrived at in the course of the poem. Keats had been working hard at it for some time, and his conclusion is proclaimed from the outset instead of emerging from the materials of its composition. The poem thus lacks the dynamic of 'Urn' and 'Nightingale', with their sense of a supple and muscular intelligence grappling with intractable elements. Nor does it display the halcyon harmony, the feeling of a hard-won serenity, that emanates from 'To Autumn'.

Part of the reason for the sense of something missing from 'Ode on Melancholy' may lie in Keats's cancelled first stanza. Some critics have interpreted the poem's present opening as a dissuasion against suicide. But a perusal of Keats's cancelled introduction, which describes the macabre preparations for a grisly voyage embarked on in order to find 'the Melancholy', reveals that his initial warning is not against suicidal tendencies but against the late-eighteenth-century cult of 'Sensibility', which recommended that the 'melancholy fit' should be actively sought for the exquisite feeling of generalised sorrow that it induced. The original first stanza sets the scene for an expedition in search of gloomy experiences; and it is the spurious value of such an enterprise that provokes Keats to spurn it so vehemently in the opening line of the revised version as it stands.

Keats had come to the belief that life is meaningless without sorrow. Melancholy energetically cultivated (not nursed in a superficial or sentimental way) lends a richer texture, a deeper hue to all experience. In order for it to expand the soul most effectively, it must not be looked for in moods of sad rumination but at the height of gay activity, when it is liable to drop unexpectedly on a mind fully aroused by stimuli of a contrary tendency (as the ecstasy of the listener to the bird's song in 'Nightingale' spills over into a 'drowsy/ numbness' akin to melancholy). 'Nor let . . . the death-moth be/ Your mournful Psyche' suggests that too deliberate a contemplation of reminders of death – the meditation on the *memento mori* of earlier centuries – will numb the soul so that it does not feel the pain of the 'melancholy fit' as sharply as it ought to do if any spiritual development is to be reaped from it: 'For shade to shade will come too drowsily,/And drown the wakeful anguish of the soul'. Not only suffering but the full awareness of such suffering ('wakeful anguish') must be borne in order for the 'identity' of the individual soul to be forged. Melancholy is therefore venerated, as if she were a goddess with a 'shrine' and 'mysteries', because she is just as essential a component in the make-up of the growing soul as are Mars and Venus, deities of the bellicose and amatory instincts.

Melancholy brings ambiguous gifts, 'cloudy trophies', a practice like that of the 'weeping cloud' whose 'shroud' of deathly tears that covers the landscape like a pall also provides renewal and continuity to the 'green hill' of life, perhaps through a purging catharsis that evacuates old dead emotion. Depression can be productive, as long as it is not simply the channelling of energy in a completely negative direction (like Spenser's figure of Despair), the option rejected in the first stanza.

Sorrow and beauty inform each other. Beauty is rendered more beautiful by the observer's awareness of its fragile durability: the rose is a 'morning' rose destined to last half a day only, the 'rainbow' of the salt sand-wave is ephemeral by nature and the 'mistress' displays a variety of moods, not all of them entrancing. In order for sorrow to instruct the soul it needs to be included in every exposure to more pleasurable objects, for pleasure without pain is mere hedonism, offering physical gratification but no spiritual enrichment. There is the paradoxical inference that melancholy is an even more refined, though painful, pleasure than pleasure itself, because it is at the root of all pleasure ('in the very temple of Delight/Veiled Melancholy has her sovran shrine') and only the connoisseur of life, the one prepared to delve 'deep, deep' into its mysteries, will ever succeed in extracting its nugget from the merely meretricious, if superficially pleasurable, coating. The discovery of his mortality will heighten his appreciation of the beautiful things that share his fate, so that he feels joy and sadness, pleasure and pain, in a simultaneous insightful moment of melancholy.

Melancholy herself remains an obscure, 'veiled' goddess. The final impression left by her personification, amid the clutter of her cloudy trophies, is of a cool aloofness from humanity. She hovers with a detached immutability over the changeable mortal creatures who visit her shrine. There is an abstract quality about this central symbol, rendering impossible the kind of easy discourse with her that Keats had been able to conduct with the more accessible and communicative central symbols of 'Urn' and 'Nightingale'. Keats is moving out of the realm of things human towards the world of pure impersonal abstractions that he discovered in 'The Fall of Hyperion'.

2.3.5 'Ode To Autumn'

Summary

The poem begins with a catalogue of some of early autumn's most celebrated features, with emphasis on its being the time of fruition in nature when orchards are delivering their crops of fruit and nuts and the flowers continue to lure the overworked bees with prodigal supplies of nectar.

Autumn is further characterised in stanza 2 through some of the activities typically associated with it: separating the wheat from the chaff ('winnowing') after the harvest, reaping the grain itself and gathering ('gleaning') the leftovers and turning apples into cider. These are all labours that are performed easily, responsibilities that are borne lightly ('careless'), by comparison with the heavy work that has preceded them. Autumn is a holiday season.

It is also a time for reflection, and stanza 3, focusing on a later stage of autumn, considers the transience of all things natural, noting how rapidly one season melts into another and how everything is in a state of flux. The lambs of spring are already 'full-grown', the bird of winter ('red-breast') has established his dominion in the garden while his less hardy companions are busy making last-minute preparations for flight to warmer climes. The sounds of animals, insects and birds combine in a chorus that is more solemn perhaps than the 'songs of Spring', but no less natural and no less harmonious.

Commentary

The last of Keats's major odes, 'To Autumn' was written at Winchester in mid-September 1819. It is imbued with tranquillity and a sense of repose, of acceptance and enjoyment of life as it is. Keats is no longer straining at the impossible task of uniting temporal and eternal worlds: he now celebrates the fallen world and his own share in its inheritance.

There is no central organising symbol in this ode, and the attributes and activities of autumn that are detailed need not be read as metaphors. They are what they are, and they simply accumulate until a clear composite picture of the season is presented. This is Keats's most 'naturalistic' poem. He is recording impressions calmly, 'without . . . fever' (as he described his aims at this time to George). Even so, his depiction is selective. Apart from the dubious benevolence of 'mists' (which Keats with his persistent sore throat had good reason to fear), the qualities of autumn that he presents are all positive ones. The poem is replete with nutritious substance, like a church at harvest festival. The less benign aspects of autumn are glossed over, though they begin to protrude above the surface in stanza 3.

The poem's subject is nature, but it is nature domesticated by man. Its trees are not wild but grow in a 'cottage' garden, perhaps the same one in which the robin ultimately sings. The vines donot straggle after their own inclination, but are carefully trained to embrace their owner's house. All the poem's images of abundance are rich only in so far as they relate to man. If the hazel shells have been plumped, it is for man's benefit and the final bird, animal and insect songs possess meaning not in themselves but in the mind of the human being who hears them.

Commonly in Keats autumn is associated with a mood of serenity, because activity is ended and a time for taking stock ensues. The image of 'autumn suns/Smiling at eve upon the quiet sheaves' (from 'After dark vapours have oppressed our plains') indicates the general mood of mute contentment, rest after labour, that autumn brings to Keats's mind. It is the time when life's development comes to a fulness – 'more generous to me than autumn sun/To ripening harvests', says Albert of Otho (*Otho the Great*, IV, i, 167–8) – when even death itself is seen to be a part of the natural pattern, and not necessarily a grim one. The essential thing is that the individual life should bear its 'fruit' before it is cut down, and perhaps Keats, when composing this poem late in his career, felt confident that he had by now written enough to ensure a golden harvest would be gleaned by future 'hungry generations' from his poetic crop ('I shall be among the English poets after my death', he had written to George the previous autumn).

The first stanza is replete with images of overabundance – the cottage-trees 'bent' with apples, all fruit filled 'with ripeness to the core', 'more, and still more' flowers set budding and the bees' cells 'o'er-brimming' with honey – and of pregnancy ('To swell the gourd, and plump the hazel shells/With a sweet kernel'), to suggest not only that the world is teeming with life, but that it is about to offer the germ of a spiritual truth ('a sweet kernel') to him who has thus far endured its seasonal and climatic vicissitudes. The physical plenitude of stanza 1 prepares for the possibility that something spiritual is about to bud out of it.

The figures in stanza 2 are both human and mythical. The humans are in that state of indolence ('Drowsed with the fume of poppies') that Keats recommended as conducive to the first, passive phase of poetic creation, when impressions from within and without are floating freely in the mind's condensing chamber. The four figures are linked by verbs suggesting continuous immobility ('sitting', 'sparing', 'keeping', 'watching'). By simultaneously using these fi-gures as personifications of autumn, Keats raises them out of their transient human bodies and eternises them, so that they assume mythological significance, even, in the second figure, admitting the presence of death itself. But this is a kindly death, not an interloper; not the grim reaper, but one of the workers and as much a part of the natural scene as any of them, even having the grace to arrest the progress of his scythe and spare for a few moments longer the late flowers that have bloomed in the previous stanza. By this fusion of the human and the mythical Keats is illuminating the significance of ordinary tasks, which normally appear only as drudgery, while humanising what is usually feared and dreaded, making of death a friend and companion. He is transmuting the sublime into the beautiful.

By the third stanza the Indian 'Summer' of stanza 1 has faded and the 'fruitfulness' engendered by the 'maturing sun' is replaced by empty fields, 'stubble-plains' and the signs of imminent depar-ture – the 'swallows' from England, and the sun's light and heat from the face of the earth. It is, though, a gentle parting, and the day disappears painlessly ('soft-dying'). The sun, in taking leave of the land, seems to plant a farewell kiss on it, to 'touch the stubble-plains with rosy hue'. Even the clouds behind which the sun is setting seem to 'bloom' with fresh life. All previous pain and conflict is here subsumed, absorbed in nature's mighty pattern. The 'wind' that 'lives or dies' parallels the fragile breath of earth's human occupants, without any heart-rending or soul-searching. The 'wailful choir' of the mourning gnats ushers in a note of ceremonial endorsement, of religious sanction to the latter end of the natural cycle. The unde-monstrative hymn of the gnats is followed by other bird, animal and insect noises that attest both to life's general continuity and to its particular ephemerality. Within the vegetable (stanza 1) and animal (stanza 3) borders to the poem a humankind that is both earthy and mythological is embedded in the central stanza, implicitly suggesting an anthropocentric universe. And, just as autumn is glimpsed and yet 'not seen' in that central stanza, its shape quickly resolving itself into a picturesque human figure, so is the comforting sense of a purpose beyond life almost, but not quite, palpable in the unfolding of the stanzas.

The solace that is drawn from the poem comes from its successful fusion of several elements: a sureness of metrical control whereby the couplet of the penultimate two lines suspends the development until the final eleventh line can conclude with an emphatic éclat, a near-perfect marriage between meaning and prosody (shown, for example, in the physical repletion – the smacking of lips – suggested by the accumulated 'm's in the first stanza) and the pervasive sense of regeneration. The roundabout phrase (or periphrasis) of 'full-grown lambs' instead of the straightforward 'sheep' serves as a reminder not only of what the animals were but of what, through their offspring, they will be, encouraging the belief that out of death comes new life, a spiritual rebirth, just as the 'oozing' of the fallen apples produces the heady new brew of cider. Keats eschews the formulation of a conventionally religious consolatory message, but his poem, in a manner almost pagan, greets the spirit of nature, the invisible core ('sweet kernel') of life, and could be read as the most implicitly optimistic of all his poems about what he called in one his last letters 'another Life'.

3 THEMES AND ISSUES

3.1 SENSUOUSNESS AND SPIRITUALITY

Keats possessed a remarkable capacity for identifying with other
people, birds, even inanimate objects. This was a sensuous identification, an instinctive understanding of the 'feelings' of the object under
his scrutiny, be it a person, a sparrow or a billiard ball (Woodhouse
reported that Keats could 'conceive of a billiard ball that it may have
a sense of delight from its own roundness, smoothness, volubility and
the rapidity of its motion'). He at once comprehended what he called
the 'countenance or intellectual tone' – what Gerard Manley Hopkins later termed the 'inscape', the unique hidden character – of
every living or non-living thing, and 'felt' the world vicariously
through sympathetic identification.

In his early poetry Keats showed an inclination to swoon in a kind
of sensual euphoria in which intellectual paralysis threatened to strike
him as he surrendered to the influence of a natural beauty, a work of
poetry – 'When some melodious sorrow spells mine eyes' (from 'O!
how I love, on a fair summer's eve') – or an affectionate ge-
sture – 'My sense with their deliciousness was spelled' ('To a Friend
who sent me some Roses'). But this was a temptation that he soon
learned to control, realising its unproductive narcissism. Though he
appreciated sensuous luxury, and his poetry is full of feasts for the
tongue, ear and eye (the banquets at crucial points in 'Lamia' and
'The Eve of St Agnes' being obvious examples), there is no indication
that he over-indulged himself personally. His is rather the palate of
the epicure, discriminating and appreciative, and sharpened by
abstinence. He might admit to George that 'whenever I can have
claret I must drink it', but this is immediately qualified by ''tis the
only palate affair that I am at all sensual in' (letter of 14 February – 3
May 1819). In a latter letter to his brother he wrote, 'I am becoming
accustomed to the privation of the pleasures of sense. In the midst of
the world I live like a hermit' (17–27 September 1819).

Keats was aware, in his life and his poetry, of the perils of sensual delights. The ambivalence contained in physical pleasure – the threat that it might cloy and turn to disgust – appears throughout Keats's work, often through his use of the image of honey, 'Turning to poison while the bee-mouth sips' ('Ode on Melancholy'), and reveals his awareness that the indulgence of sensual appetites is not enough. The 'soul' risks getting 'lost in pleasant smotherings', as he says in 'I stood tip-toe'. The disciplined rejection of the world of luxuries became increasingly central to Keats's life, partly from necessity, partly from conviction. Eventually he was to prefer the 'beautiful' prospect of 'the blank side of a house' in Winchester to 'the view of the sea from our window at Shanklin' (letter to Fanny Brawne, 16 August 1819). This willing privation of the senses had earlier been expressed in the 'Grecian Urn' ode: 'Heard melodies are sweet, but those unheard/ Are sweeter'.

The purpose of sensuousness in Keats's poetry is to stimulate the soul, not 'smother' it. The concept of the 'pleasure thermometer', explained to Taylor on 30 January 1818, sees happiness as growing from joy in natural phenomena, through pleasure in music and poetry, to friendship and love and becoming progressively more spiritual. In the course of this ascending journey the soul learns that pleasure cannot be 'unperplexed' from 'its neighbour pain' ('Lamia', I, 192). The intenser the joy, the sharper the pain, as 'Ode on Melancholy' attests, and as the goddess Diana acknowledges when she revives the swooned Endymion with a kiss: 'O bliss! O pain!' (*Endymion*, II, 773). Pleasure and pain, both of which are experienced through the senses ('on the pulses', in Keats's phrase), are steps in the schooling of the soul, grades that it must pass through.

The soul needs the body to instigate it on its spiritual journey. Without physical beauty a more refined love would be impossible. Without it there could be no spiritual devotion, as Keats indicated to Fanny Brawne: 'I cannot conceive any beginning of such love as I have for you but Beauty' (8 July 1819). Sensuous experience and spiritual vitality are inseparably interconnected. The spirit could not develop without the physically acquired knowledge of joy and suffering. And sensual pleasures, unleavened by spiritual essence, soon satiate and turn stale. 'Where's the voice, however soft,/One would hear so very oft?' asks Keats in 'Fancy'.

Uniting these strands together is Keats's idea, formulated late in his life, but perhaps implicit in his earliest 'swoonings', that death might be the supreme sensual pleasure. A sonnet of 1819, 'Why did I laugh tonight?', concludes by declaring

> Verse, Fame, and Beauty are intense indeed,
> But Death intenser – Death is Life's high meed.

possibly punning on 'mead' (an intoxicating drink made from honey), as if death were to be quaffed with gusto. Keats might have been turning towards death as the grand absorber of life's contradictions and frustrations, the annihilator of 'mortal pain', as well as the terminator of pleasure. And perhaps the great sleep of non-existence would be the most exquisite of all pleasures, Hamlet's consummation devoutly to be wished ('I . . . relish Hamlet more than I ever have done', he wrote to Reynolds a year before). Eventually frustrations both private and professional brought Keats close to the point of feeling that it might, after all, be rich to die. 'I have two luxuries to brood over in my walks', he wrote to Fanny on 25 July 1819, 'your loveliness and the hour of my death. O that I could have possession of them both in the same minute'.

3.2 LOVE, SUFFERING AND IMMORTALITY

Keats came to believe that love was inseparable from suffering and that both were essential elements in the soul's education. Suffering sharpens a person's self-knowledge, drawing the immortal part of him in clearer outline: it builds character. Love and suffering point the soul toward its post-mortal destination, a goal that is obscure in all of Keats's poems (Endymion, Lamia, Porphyro and Madeline all 'vanish' to a region beyond the poet's ability to follow). Keats's evocative portrayal of the tangible 'sweets' of the sensual world contrasts with his hesitancy before the 'mist' of the next world. Not that Keats was an atheist. His early poetry makes frequent reference to the invisible 'Framer' and to biblical events such as Christ's final judgement – 'When some good spirit walks upon the earth' – and depends upon its source being in a region 'where the great God lives for evermore' ('To Kosciusko'). But he seemed to fear, like Blake, that religious orthodoxy would stifle the impulse to flight of the imagination, as the philosopher lances the serpent in 'Lamia'. Religion threatened to smother the creative fire and render it inactive: 'Surely the mind of man is closely bound/In some black spell' ('Written in Disgust of Vulgar Superstition').

   Keats's last expression of a more or less conventional Christian viewpoint was in his sonnet 'To my Brothers' (November 1816), which concludes by deferring to 'the great voice' that 'shall bid our spirits fly'. His Christianity, if such it was, was henceforth unconventional if not heterodox. The 'clear religion of heaven' of Endymion (I, 781) is lucid because it is Keats's own theology (the steps from physical to spiritual pleasures), the product of imagining rather than 'consequitive' reasoning, not developed from any scriptural exegesis. In Endymion love has a redeeming quality, but it is erotic love which resurrects the drowned lovers in Book III, not the charitable love advocated by Christ. Such love as this, centred in the loved one, saves its possessors because it gives them another being to prize above themselves, so that they become 'Forgetful utterly of self-intent' (III, 386). Love ultimately conquers death, the Christian theme – 'Death fell a-weeping in his charnel-house' (III, 788) – but it is love of a secular not a spiritual object. Assurances of immortality are accordingly compromised. Significantly, though, Endymion is excluded from the joyful lovers' reunion until he has suffered enough to be 'spiritualised' – made ready for integration with his goddess. Only love and suffering together, it seems, can prepare one for an unconditional, if indistinct, eternity.

The importance of suffering as a spiritual teacher becomes more emphatic in Keats's later poetry. In mid-career Keats was almost overwhelmed by an increasing sensitivity to the world's suffering, which he could no longer exclude from his poetry. Like Tennyson later, whose melancholy brooding produced a vision of nature 'red in tooth and claw', Keats's speculations drew an equally stark image of the natural world: 'I . . . should have been most happy, – but I saw/Too far into the sea, where every maw/The greater on the less feeds evermore' ('To J. H. Reynolds, Esq.'). Keats's philosophy of the value of suffering in what he called the 'system of spirit-creation . . . to school an intelligence and make it a soul' (letter to George, 15 February 1819) applied not only to personal suffering but to suffering in sympathy with the woes of others, as Moneta spells out in 'The Fall of Hyperion'. The poet takes up the burden of the world's suffering and can no longer surrender to the charms of the nightingale's song. Only in the afterworld will he be free to hear it, with an enhanced understanding, so that it seems

> Not a senseless, trancèd thing,
> But divine melodious truth.
> ('Bards of Passion and of Mirth')

In heaven there is no body/soul dichotomy and truth and its vehicle, beauty, may be apprehended simultaneously, in entirety.

The state of this heaven, however, was conjectural and Keats wavered between belief and doubt to the end of his life. After the death of Tom, Keats wrote to his other brother George, 'I have scarce a doubt of immortality of some nature [or] other': a confidence similar to that expressed a year earlier (22 November 1817), in far different circumstances, to Bailey, to whom Keats wrote of 'that delicious face you will see', the 'Prototype' of all beauty that 'must' be beheld in the life to come. At other times, particularly as his own demise loomed over him, Keats saw death as the portal to nothing-ness, as Joseph Severn remarked: 'this noble fellow lying on the bed – is dying in horror – no kind hope smoothing down his suffering – no philosophy to support him'. Keats confronted the issue in one of his last letters to Brown (30 September 1820): 'Is there another Life? Shall I awake and find all this a dream? There must be; we cannot be created for this sort of suffering'. At times Keats's honest scepticism borders upon the existentialism of the twentieth century: 'I scarcely remember counting upon any happiness – I look not for it if it be not in the present hour – nothing startles me beyond the moment' (letter to Bailey, 22 November 1817). This yielding of himself to the primacy of the present moment is part and parcel of Keats's lack of a settled doctrine, Christian or otherwise.

Keats's poetry fluctuates between joy and sorrow, between love and suffering, attempting with incomplete success to fuse them into a spiritual entity, a soul equipped for an indeterminate paradise. From his last reflective poems, 'To Autumn' and 'The Fall of Hyperion', emanates a readiness to accept life as it really is; and one of its realities is the inconclusive evidence of a world beyond this one, and hence the uncertainty as to whether love and suffering serve the end of refining the individual's better qualities, or have simply to be enjoyed or endured for their own sakes.

3.3 POETIC VISION

One indication that there is an eternal region of spiritual verity was, for Keats, the activity of the poetic imagination. This faculty enables its possessor to 'think divinely' (Epistle 'To my Brother George'), opening up for him the 'portal' to the 'golden halls' of beautiful truth inaccessible to less gifted individuals. Admittance into this ethereal zone comes suddenly, often after much 'striving'. The privileged 'flashes' (in Wordsworth's expression) of poetic vision illuminate, if briefly, the obscurities of the other world, so that 'In air he sees white coursers paw, and prance'. Once he has caught such visions in his language, the poet immediately sloughs off his 'melancholy fit' ('Ode on Melancholy'), becomes sprightly and jocular and can contemplate even his death with equanimity ('Now more than ever seems it rich to die': 'Ode to a Nightingale'), assured that he has captured some crystal of numinous worth that will enrich future generations avid for spiritual treasures. The intimations of immortality seemingly vouchsafed by the thrilling visitations of poetic vision probably account for the strongly positive streak in Keats's poetry.

On the other hand, poetic vision could not be depended upon to come when called. In Wordsworth it faded in his early middle age ('Whither is fled the visionary gleam?' he wrote at the age of 32); in Keats its appearance was erratic and unpredictable, and it was sometimes absent for weeks together. At such times the intoxicating sureness which had borne the poet along on chargers of inspiration,

'O'er-sailing the blue cragginess' ('Sleep and Poetry'), is replaced by muddied doubt and confusion, the ecstasy of earlier visions now seeming merely a deluded evasion of sordid reality. The terrible notion presents itself that the 'wide portal' thrown open by the efforts of imagination may yawn on emptiness ('would bear along/My soul to nothingness'). Occasions when inspiration had the sulks and 'no dream arises' ('On Receiving a Laurel Crown from Leigh Hunt') arose throughout Keats's career. Typically, Keats turned them to advantage by making them not only the subject of his poetry but important elements in his continuing discussion with himself as to whether poetry really was divinely guided or whether it merely provided a decorative covering to 'a dizzy void' ('Sleep and Poetry').

This perpetual debate is evidenced in one of Keat's minor sonnets, 'Read me a lesson, Muse, and speak it loud', written on his Scottish tour. Surrounded by mist on the summit of Ben Nevis, Keats has relapsed into one of his groping, dismal moods, when he himself is suffering from the vapours, a fall of confidence when the 'inward sight' seems to be blind, a Hopkins-like depression when the 'mind has mountains' and even the effort of poetic creation offers no hope of a breakthrough into the 'pure serene' of clearer vision ('all my eye doth meet/Is mist and crag'). Keats's dilemma is apparent, his preference wavering between supreme confidence in the ability of poetry to soar above all the dark 'chasms' of the psyche, and a sudden hesitation prompted by the acknowledgement of man's limitless capacity for self-deception, whence fancy and imagination may be no better than delusion and hallucination. If poetry is not divinely inspired, then the truth suggested by its beauty is a chimera, its effect not positive but pernicious. A suspicion such as this may have been in Keats's mind when he wrote to Charles Dilke (on 22 September 1819), 'I have no trust whatever on poetry . . . the marvel is to me how people read so much of it'.

Despite recurrent doubts, however, poetry remained the essential core of Keats's life. 'I cannot exist without poetry', he wrote to Reynolds (18 April 1817), and to his brother George 18 months later, 'I live under an everlasting restraint – never relieved except when I am composing' (16 December 1818). Poetry was a 'demon' which drove him on, shortening his life, he believed ('I feel from my employment that I shall never be again secure in robustness': letter to Bailey, 8 October 1818). Poetic creation demands struggle; it will not drop ready-made into the lap of him who simply and passively 'pillows his head on the sweets of the rose'.

At the same time, though, an 'indolent' frame of mind is conducive to receptivity, the primary stage of the creative act. This is an idea to which Keats spirals back from time to time. To nurse daydreams or, like the personified 'Autumn' in the ode, to meditate in drowsy immobility is not to 'idle' one's time away; for in such a state comes 'knowledge', intuitional rather than institutional, not the knowledge of books but the understanding of the blood: 'he's awake who thinks himself asleep' ('O thou whose face hath felt the Winter's wind'). 'Indolence' seems to be a state of relaxation, halfway between consciousness and the heightened awareness ('Surely I dreamt today, or did I see/ . . . with awakened eyes?': 'Ode to Psyche') of dreams. In indolence ideas float around in the poet's mind like half-formed images, in embryonic forms and undefined relationships, before he has 'strained his nerves' (letter to Mary-Ann Jeffery, 31 May 1819) to organise a poem out of them. It is the passive 'state of effeminacy', a necessary prelude to the active masculine state of energetic composition.

Poetic inspiration comes either from heaven or from the unconscious, from external or internal spiritual springs. A third source is the interaction between general nature and individual imagination:

> My bowl is the sky,
> And I drink at my eye,
> Till I feel in the brain
> A Delphian pain.
> ('Hence Burgundy, Claret, and Port')

The final reference to 'pain' is a reminder of the labour and endurance required in giving birth to a poem, as well as the exhilaration derived from the travail. In the course of this labour, truth may be created extempore, grasped and moulded from the inspiration of the moment: 'what the imagination seizes as beauty must be truth – whether it existed before or not' (letter to Bailey, 22 November 1817).

The subject of much of Keats's poetry, sometimes hidden beneath layers of narrative or meditation, is poetry itself, its transformative power over experience. In this perspective Lycius's infatuation with Lamia, who, like poetry, is able to shrink life's tedious hours (to make 'the triple league decrease/To a few paces': I, 345–6)and expand its significant moments, is a false relationship with a poetic vision from which pain has been excluded. The comprehensive vision accepts everything, aware that life's purpose ends in death, finding its most complete expression in 'To Autumn'. 'Poesy' is the word Keats uses to indicate an insufficient poetic vision, an escapist illusion like that of Lycius or that of his own early verse. Even in his formative years, however, he realised that he would sooner or later have to plunge into that 'muddy stream', the obscure source and end of life and death, and struggle subaqueously like Endymion in the hope of reaching 'a gleaming through the tide' (III, 718), an understanding of life's darker purposes and humanity's place among them.

3.4 NEGATIVE CAPABILITY

Keats's initial inability to forge for himself a philosophy through which to view the world was eventually turned into an advantage. He realised that his moral uncertainty left him free to explore all subjects, all human natures, without any preconceived or prejudiced opinions. This anti-philosophical approach was explained in a letter to his brothers (21 December 1817) and given the name of 'negative capability'. It depends on the faculty 'of remaining content with half-knowledge', of not attempting to impose an explanation on all the phenomena that come before conscious awareness, the protean shapes given temporary form by the borrowed robes of language. 'The only means of strengthening one's intellect', said Keats in a later letter to George (17–27 September 1819), 'is to make up one's mind about nothing – to let the mind be a thoroughfare for all thoughts'. The fostering of this attitude in himself liberated Keats. It allowed him to write though lacking a moral centre, a philosophical system, or even a clear theme for his poetry. Its moral content would be discovered and divulged in the course of working out the poem, as the odes exemplify.

Negative capability encouraged sympathetic identification with the object of contemplation and a consequent transcendence of the self – it encouraged an objective (what Keats called 'disinterested') rather than a subjective approach to life. 'I/Have no self-passion or identity', says Endymion (IV, 476–7), rehearsing in verse Keats's prose formulation of the concept.

Keats held that the defining quality of 'men of genius' was that 'they have not any individuality, any determined character' (letter to Bailey, 22 November 1817). They had instead an 'intensity' of insight that enabled them to sympathise with alien natures. From this point of view all experience is grist to the poet's mill. He has no preference, nor can he apply moral censorship to what he writes. His task is simply to expose life in all its variegated texture, to record its lights and shadows indiscriminately: 'Infant playing with a skull;/Morning fair, and stormwrecked hull' ('Welcome joy, and welcome sorrow'). Negative capability is what supplies the poet with his 'chameleon' camouflage, able to adapt to suit any environment: 'The poetical character . . . has no self – it is every thing and nothing' (letter to Woodhouse, 27 October 1818). The poet 'has no character' of his own for he assumes the character of the whole universe.

Given his commitment to universal nature, the poet must overrule his personal inclinations. Keats's compassion always went out to the artist who sacrificed his own urges in order to transmit his spiritual findings. The poet altruistically pioneers new spiritual territory and magnanimously shares his enlightenment with all. The personal life must be subordinate to the demands of the poetic mission, as Keats emphasised by absenting himself from Fanny Brawne in the summer of 1819, promising her at best only a fleeting visit (which he never fulfilled), 'for as I am in a train of writing now, I fear to disturb it' (letter to Fanny, 5 August 1819).

Having negative capability meant ignoring the demands of one's own flesh, which threatened to disturb the flow of ideas and disrupt the poetic vision, as Keats realised: 'a few more moments' thought of you would uncrystallise and dissolve me – I must not give way to it – but turn to my writing again' (letter to Fanny, 16 August 1819). In a late poem, 'What can I do to drive away', Keats acknowledges the conflict between his love for Fanny and his poetic ambitions: the former is a 'snare' to trap the erstwhile 'soaring' poet. The lure of carnal temptation is one to which Lycius succumbs in 'Lamia'. Towards the end of Keats's life, when he had virtually stopped writing poetry, the temptation seems to have become too strong for him as well: 'You have absorbed me. I have a sensation at the present as though I was dissolving' (letter to Fanny, 13 October 1819).

For most of his career, however, Keats was able to operate from the impersonal base of his negative capability. This sometimes resulted in disagreeable side-effects on his personal life. The ability to sympthise readily with another's sufferings could become oppressive, inviting the weight of the other's personality to impose itself too obtrusively. Sustained contact even with someone Keats loved could prove intolerable: '[Tom's] identity pressed upon me so all day that I am obliged to go out' (letter to Dilke, 20 September 1818). The ideal would be to cultivate negative capability for the professional poetic life, retaining a personal identity for private use. Sometimes Keats was able to do this, his poetic soul uniting with the singing nightingale or picking about the gravel with the sparrow outside his window, while in his personal capacity he felt no compunction at regarding birds as legitimate prey for the sportsman: 'I went with Dilke a-shooting on the heath and shot a tom-tit' (letter to George Keats, 16 December 1818).

At the end of his career Keats went beyond the standpoint of negative capability, coming ultimately to regard it as irresponsible, the guise of the dreamer not the true poet, who must also be a philosopher. In 'The Fall of Hyperion' he accepts the burden of moral responsibility. The equal 'delight in creating and Iago or an Imogen' in amoral indifference is replaced by an agreement to bear the 'miseries of the world' as if they were his own. Since Keats had also by this time come to believe that fine doing was preferable to fine writing, that benefaction was superior to eloquence, perhaps his next logical step, after finally abandoning his 'Hyperion' drafts, would have been to turn aside from poetry altogether.

4 TECHNIQUES

4.1 IMAGERY

Keats's images are celebrated for the strong impression they leave on the senses. There is a richness which amounts to luxury in the early verse, a cloying sweetness that Keats soon recognised and attempted to purge from his post-*Endymion* poetry, realising that such 'honied' abundance can turn 'to poison'. The images, though less profuse, remain sharply sensuous, as if Keats were determined to attack two or three senses at the same time:

> The coming musk-rose, full of dewy wine,
> The murmurous haunt of flies on summer eves.
> ('Ode to a Nightingale')

Scent ('musk'), taste ('wine'), texture ('dewy') and colour ('rose') are all suggested in the first line, with which the 'm's, 'u's and 's's of the second line interweave to implant an impression on the fifth sense (of sound): the lazy buzzing of insects at twilight time.

So keen was Keats on stimulating multi-sensual responses that he often used the device of synaesthesia, whereby the faculties of one sense are attributed to another to which they do not properly belong. Thus in 'Ode to a Nightingale' incense 'hangs' as if smells had the density of solid objects, the mouth is endowed with sight in *Endymion* ('dazzled lips': IV, 419) and sounds have colours ('speak not one pale word': IV, 808). Lamia's feast is 'teeming with odours' (II, 133), Saturn's ear usurps the function of his palate and is 'all a-hungered' ('Hyperion', II, 163), while in the same poem sound engineers colour for the eye when music 'leaves the dinned air vibrating silverly' (II, 128).

The same technique appears in Keats's letters. To his sister, for example, he describes some flowers, the sight of which is so delicious that it stimulates the taste buds: 'violets . . . in a shower of rain are almost as fine as barley sugar drops are to a schoolboy's tongue' (12 April 1819). In a letter to Taylor he combines impressions of sight, smell and taste in one image to give his subject as much physical presence as possible: 'the autumn fogs over a rich land is like steam from cabbage water' (5 September 1819). Often the poet is able, by such means, to forget himself, to lose himself by imaginative transference to the image he is shaping, thereby dulling his aches and pains into oblivion. Image-creating could become a drug, and therein lay its danger.

In a sonnet written in 1818, 'Time's sea hath been five years at its slow ebb', Keats draws attention to his method of misappropriating the functions of the several senses: 'my fond ear, in fancy at thy lips,/ . . . doth devour/Its sweets in the wrong sense'. The last three words are perhaps an admission on the part of Keats that some transgression – of moral, physical or aesthetic laws – is involved in the use of synaesthesia. It allows one sense to trespass on the territory of another, distorting the physical reality that Keats became more and more concerned to put into his poetry.

By the time he was writing 'The Fall of Hyperion' the resolution to resist the temptation to wallow in luxurious imagery had been firmly taken. The course of the verse, though it might for a while meander like 'Ode to a Nightingale' among the luscious vegetation of grass, thicket and fruit-tree wild, returns repeatedly and inexorably to the speaker's 'sole self'. He is no longer content to set negative capability in motion and lose himself in his imagery. After finding himself initially in the familiar sensual paradise of 'Palm, myrtle, oak, and sycamore', lulled by the splash of 'fountains', regaled by a waft of 'scent', not far from roses', amid the remnants of a sumptuous feast ('fragrant husks and berries crushed'), the speaker eventually stands deprived of all physical props, forced back entirely on his own spiritual resources, unable even to receive sense-impressions of his own body ('when I clasped my hands I felt them not': I, 131).

Keats finally rejected rich imagery in favour of a stark confrontation with the physical and psychological essence of the human condition. Like his dreamer in 'The Fall of Hyperion' he had at last stopped striving 'hard to escape' (I, 127) from the hard reality of earthly life into a charmed magic land opened up by the imaginative deployment of imagery. This ultimately austere development in Keats is outlined in miniature in his maturest ode, 'To Autumn', where the lush superabundance of pregnant imagery in the first stanza gives way to the 'dying' sensual impressions of the third, ending in a diminuendo of bird-song that bids farewell to gorgeous imagery as well as to the generosity of summer.

4.2 DICTION

Keats's early poetry betrays his dependence, during his apprentice-ship, on models both past and present. The archaisms that Spenser deliberately incorporated in *The Faerie Queene* to lend an air of distance and dream to its chivalric ambience find their way, with less justification, into Keats's verse. Words like 'teen' (sorrow), 'bedight' (adorned) and 'bale' (misery) crop up frequently, along with the vocabulary of knightly contest: 'tournament', 'banneral', 'plumes', 'lance', 'courser', and so on. Keats's mature poetry is not immune from attacks of Spenserian diction, as the 'shielded scutcheon' of 'The Eve of St Agnes' and the antique spelling of 'faery lands' in 'Ode to a Nightingale' bear witness. By this time, though, the medievalism suggested by such language has an organic place in the thematic argument, and is no longer being summoned by Keats for the mere frisson it gives – the thrill of making superficial contact with an idealised territory – which is its sole *raison d'être* in much of the early work: a gratuitous revelling in a magic land for no deeper purpose than to beguile the present moment ('Lo! I must tell a tale of chivalry;/For large white plumes are dancing in mine eye': 'Specimen of an Induction to a Poem'). By the time Keats came to write 'La Belle Dame sans Merci' his 'knight-at-arms' is no longer simply a picturesque chevalier like the hero of the juvenile 'Calidore' ('burning/To hear of knightly deeds'), but a metaphor for one whose quest is all-consuming, exhaustive and deadly. The diction is not now there for its quaintness; it has an integral role to play in indicating the layers of meaning.

A less profitable influence on Keats's diction was his contemporary Leigh Hunt, who in 'The Story of Rimini' affected a sort of Regency Spenserianism to create a specious Faerie Queeneland. Keats copied Hunt in the use of adjectives, many of them newly coined, ending in 'y' ('bloomy', 'shadowy'), adverbs formed by adding 'ly' to the present participle ('lingeringly', 'droopingly'), the use of nouns as if they were verbs ('joy not too much'), the formation of nouns from present participles ('curious bending', 'yellow flutterings') and an irresistible urge to wallow among words of sensual luxury ('delicious', 'sweet delight', 'lush', 'dewiness', 'amorous and fondling nips', 'ravishment'). This reliance on Huntian diction lends an air of preciosity, of disingenuous coyness, to much of Keats's early verse, and was to continue up to *Endymion* with its 'slippery blisses' (II, 758). But such artificial diction is often counterpointed by crystal-clear vocabulary and unadorned imagery. In 'I stood tip-toe', for instance, among the plethora of Huntian extravaganza – 'luxuries bright, milky, soft and rosy', 'pillowy silkiness' – are sprinkled unpre-tentious accurate recordings of the natural world: the minnows 'staying their wavy bodies 'gainst the streams', of whom Keats notices,

> If you but scantily hold out the hand,
> That very instant not one will remain;
> But turn your eye, and they are there again.

The diction here is Wordsworthian in its directness, 'language really used by men'. The application of plain diction to natural observation came to Keats more easily, initially, in his letters than in his poetry ('I might as well tell a hen to hold up her head before she drinks instead of afterwards': letter to Bailey, 18 July 1818).

Other influences on Keats's diction were Shakespeare and Milton. One he regarded as a blessing, the other a bane. From Shakespeare he learned compactness and concreteness: 'impassioned clay' in his 'King Lear' sonnet, with its succinct summary of man's diverse nature, part animated spirit and part mindless lump, is a good example of this. Milton taught him to use sonorous diction, Latin phrasing and epic image, discernible for example in the line from 'Hyperion', 'thunderous waterfalls and torrents hoarse' (II, 8), with its throaty assonance and its inverted noun/adjective construction at the end. Keats never felt that he could assimilate Milton's style and make it his own, as he could Shakespeare's.

From the beginning Keats's susceptibility to the influence, sometimes beneficial sometimes harmful, of other writers ancient and modern was fighting with his healthy determination to find his own voice. In *Endymion* the two tendencies exist side by side, rubbing shoulders in uneasy intimacy:

> The moon put forth a little diamond peak . . .
> Bright signal that she only stooped to tie
> Her silver sandals, ere deliciously
> She bowed into the heavens her timid head.
> (IV, 497–502)

This description of the moonrise begins with a limpid clarity that is extended into a brilliantly apt personification – one which is marred, however, by the inclusion of two words, 'deliciously' and 'timid', which align the moon with Leigh Hunt's blushing maidens and detract from its ethereal luminosity.

The gradual development in Keats's diction, the steady progress to a vocabulary cleansed of all impurities, may be traced through the growing irony in his use of the word 'Poesy' for 'poetry'. In his early verse it is employed unironically to indicate his vision of poetry as an Arcadian escape-world free of the sordid burdens of reality: 'If I do hide myself, it sure shall be/In the very fane, the light of Poesy'

('Sleep and Poetry'). But when, in 'Ode to a Nightingale', he talks of becoming intoxicated 'on the viewless wings of Poesy', the ironic juxtaposition of the word with the wine-god Bacchus is a rueful acknowledgement that 'the fancy' cannot sustain such an escape beyond a few fleeting moments, as the rest of the poem bears out. The ironic resonance of 'Poesy' now recognises that the flight to the nightingale's habitat 'among the leaves' is a mere 'cheat'. Reality must be faced sooner or later, at which point 'Poesy' will become 'poetry', the dreamer will graduate to the rank of poet, as promised in 'The Fall of Hyperion'. In this, the last of Keat's serious poems, 'Poesy' is unambiguously portrayed as the craft of the mere 'dreamer' ('For Poesy alone can tell her dreams': I, 8), a false practice, a 'spell', holding the dreamer in an enchanted world of unreality. Now at last 'Poesy' and all its alluring impedimenta of evocative diction must be pared down to the starkest of statements, as the diction of the first 'Hyperion' is shorn of much of its 'fine excess' in its revised form. The final stage in Keats's evolving relationship with words was (to adapt a phrase from 'Isabella') to cut language with a sharp knife to the bone.

4.3   METRE AND SOUND-EFFECTS

The ability to enhance an exact observation of nature with a metrical echo seemed to have come intuitively to Keats, and is evident from his earliest poetry:

> thĕ déer's swíft léap
> Stártlĕs thĕ wĭld bée frŏm thĕ fóxglŏve béll. ('O Solitude')

The spondee (´´)that ends the first line, the trochees (´˘) that intrude upon the second, then the resumed iambic (˘´) metre all contribute to the picture of the feeding insect momentarily disturbed by a nervous animal before settling once more to its task. Keats also displayed a natural tendency to write onomatopoeically, settling as if by instinct upon words which, separately or in combination, sound like what they signify:

> he had felt too much for such harsh jars.
> (*Endymion*, II, 865)

Here the final spondee, with its two long 'ā' vowels broken by two fricatives ('sh', 'j') requiring a glottal stop to separate them, imitates the ugliness of sound, the 'rough-voiced war' of Endymion's futile complaints at this point.

Keats was even able to conjure the sound of silence:

> A little noiseless noise among the leaves.
> ('I stood tip-toe')

The susurration of the sibilant 's' and liquid 'l' consonants creates a hushed, listening effect, a tactic deployed again later on in 'Hyperion':

> Not so much life as on a summer's day
> Robs not one light seed from the feathered grass,
> But where the dead leaf fell, there did it rest.
> (I, 8–10)

By this time Keats had embellished his natural gift with consciously acquired art. Interwoven with the 'l' and 's' consonants repeated 'd's and 'f's accumulate an impression of muted finality, while recurring vowel sounds, particularly the flat 'ĕ' in 'feathered', 'where', 'dead', 'fell', 'there' and 'rest' pile up to inflict upon the reader's ear a sense of airless stagnation. Alliteration and assonance are working in perfect unison: clipped consonants and closed vowels exactly convey the listlessness of Saturn's fallen house, where no sound can be prolonged because there is no life or spirit to sustain it.

After 'Hyperion' Keats was able to exploit his concerted mastery of assonance, alliteration and metre at will. Possibly by luck, but more probably by judgement, the various metres chosen by Keats for his mature narratives and odes turned out to be perfectly suited to the subjects they had to carry. 'The Eve of St Agnes', with the delaying effect of its Alexandrine at the end of each stanza, 'freezes' the action at certain key points so that the kinetic medium of poetry becomes for a time the static art of painting:

> With hair blown back,
> and wings put cross-wise on their breasts.'

This technique encourages contemplation, the extra foot imposing a pause for reflection, either aesthetic or moral ('She knelt, so pure a thing, so free from mortal taint'; 'Thou canst not surely be the same that thou didst seem'). 'Lamia', on the other hand, depicting a headlong and impulsive dash towards catastrophe, has no time for rumination. Its couplets proceed precipitately to its foredoomed conclusion, its occasional Alexandrines momentarily impeding but not halting the rush to disaster.

Keats's adroitness, not merely with the metre of the line but with the rhythm of the whole stanza, is seen to perfection in 'To Autumn' where, instead of the more symmetrical 10-lined stanza preferred in most of the other odes, an 11-line stanza is developed, the 'odd' line coming just before the end:

> And still more, later flowers for the bees,
> Until they think warm days will never cease,
> For summer has o'er-brimmed their clammy cells.

The unexpected 'extension' of the stanza here serves to emphasise the liberality of nature, whose bounty is so great that it requires the additional penultimate line to contain it.

There is a happy marriage between sound and sense throughout Keats's work:

> As men talk in a dream, so Corinth all . . .
> Mutter'd, like tempest in the distance brewed. ('Lamia', I, 353)

Here the onomatopoeic 'muttered' is also a trochee, breaking above the sea of surrounding iambs as the threat of surreptitious envy rises occasionally above the undertone of unsuspected spite it usually maintains. The long vowel of the final 'brewed' conveys the sense of a sustained and sullen grumbling, an impression enhanced not only by the image of distant thunder but also by the pun on 'brood': the Corinth populace is meditating its revenge on the guileless Lycius, preparing to strike his happiness with its forked lightning. A cornucopia of further examples suggests itself. In the best of Keats's work metre, sound and meaning merge with and enrich one another 'as the rose/Blendeth its odour with the violet'.

5 SPECIMEN PASSAGE AND COMMENTARY

5.1 SPECIMEN PASSAGE 'THE EVE OF ST AGNES', STANZAS XXII–XXVII

XXII

Her faltering hand upon the balustrade,
Old Angela was feeling for the stair,
When Madeline, St Agnes' charmèd maid,
Rose, like a missioned spirit, unaware:
With silver taper's light, and pious care,
She turned, and down the agèd gossip led
To a safe level matting. Now prepare,
Young Porphyro, for gazing on that bed –
She comes, she comes again, like ring-dove frayed and fled.

XXIII

Out went the taper as she hurried in;
Its little smoke, in pallid moonshine, died:
She closed the door, she panted, all akin
To spirits of the air, and visions wide:
No uttered syllable, or, woe betide!
But to her heart, her heart was voluble,
Paining with eloquence her balmy side;
As though a tongueless nightingale should swell
Her throat in vain, and die, heart-stifled, in her dell.

XXIV

A casement high and triple-arched there was,
All garlanded with carven imag'ries
Of fruits, and flowers, and bunches of knot-grass,
And diamonded with panes of quaint device,
Innumerable of stains and splendid dyes,
As are the tiger-moth's deep-damasked wings;

And in the midst, 'mong thousand heraldries,
And twilight saints, and dim emblazonings,
A shielded scutcheon blushed with blood of queens and kings.

XXV

Full on this casement shone the wintry moon,
And threw warm gules on Madeline's fair breast,
As down she knelt for heaven's grace and boon;
Rose-bloom fell on her hands, together pressed,
And on her silver cross soft amethyst,
And on her hair a glory, like a saint:
She seemed a splendid angel, newly dressed,
Save wings, for Heaven: – Porphyro grew faint;
She knelt, so pure a thing, so free from mortal taint.

XXVI

Anon his heart revives; her vespers done,
Of all its wreathèd pearls her hair she frees;
Unclasps her warmèd jewels one by one;
Loosens her fragrant bodice; by degrees
Her rich attire creeps rustling to her knees:
Half-hidden, like a mermaid in sea-weed,
Pensive awhile she dreams awake, and sees,
In fancy, fair St Agnes in her bed,
But dares not look behind, or all the charm is fled.

XXVII

Soon, trembling in her soft and chilly nest,
In sort of wakeful swoon, perplexed she lay,
Until the poppied warmth of sleep oppressed
Her soothèd limbs, and soul fatigued away –
Flown, like a thought, until the morrow-day;
Blissfully havened both from joy and pain;
Clasped like a missal where swart Paynims pray;
Blinded alike from sunshine and from rain,
As though a rose should shut, and be a bud again.

5.2 COMMENTARY

This section clarifies the poem's contrast between the generations of
'young Porphyro' and 'old Angela'. The older generation is physically
debilitated, 'faltering', the younger buoyed up by the hope, in 'dreams
awake'. In addition a distinction is drawn between the unsuspecting
innocence and vulnerability of Madeline ('like ring-dove frayed') and
the cannier character of Porphyro, whose superiority in worldly

wisdom is matched in this episode by Madeline's moral ascendancy over him.

Madeline appears throughout brim-full of spiritual quality, though not to the exclusion of physical vitality. She rises 'like a missioned spirit', as if bound for heaven by a natural proclivity, whereas the earthier Angela prefers the less giddy security of the ground floor's 'level matting'. Madeline's compassion is demonstrated by her deferring her own pleasures to attend briefly to her servant's comfort. She is a composite of human and divine elements. She is compared to a 'saint', even to an 'angel' at the gates of 'Heaven', but her less exalted physical constitution is not neglected. Her panting breath is a reminder of her mortal nature, uniting her momentarily with the lowly beadsman, whose 'frosted breath' has been depicted in stanza I. The comparison of her self-communings about the expected dream-vision to a 'tongueless nightingale' introduces an ambivalent note to the proceedings, placing Porphyro's hitherto blameless manoeuvres in the category of rape (through the myth of Philomela, ravished and rendered mute by her brother-in-law). At the same time Madeline is not absolved of all responsibility for her forthcoming seduction. Her naïve surrender to the St Agnes legend has aspects of narcissism in it, of unproductive self-absorption ('to her heart, her heart was voluble'). The solipsism of her sexual 'fancy' must be made more social. This will be the task of the real Porphyro lurking in the closet, as opposed to the unreal Porphyro nurtured by her fantasy.

At present Madeline is too virginal, imprisoned in her idealism. She is tinged by the shade of 'pallid moonshine'; but she possesses too the potential of vibrant physicality, as stanza XXIV makes clear. Here she is linked, like Porphyro before her ('a thought came like a full-blown rose,/Flushing his brow'), with natural organisms ('fruits, and flowers') and with the vital blood-red hue ('As are the tiger-moth's deep-damasked wings'), suggesting both a healthy sexuality and a princely lineage: 'A shielded scutcheon blushed with blood of queens and kings'. The image of the stained-glass window, which illuminates Madeline's bedroom, unites tradition and spontaneity – the pragmatism that prompts Madeline to fly from the family castle when dream, instinct, and practical sense, all point to the ostracised Porphyro as the next stage in her development. 'Blushed with blood' suggests a certain diffidence about the physical qualities she half-knows herself to possess (like Shakespeare's Desdemona she is 'a maiden . . . /Of spirit so still and quiet that her motion/Blush'd at herself': *Othello*, I, iii, 94–6). The richly decorated casement implies the amalgamation in Madeline's character of pagan energy ('carven imag'ries'), natural resourcefulness ('Innumerable of stains and splendid dyes') and religious sanctity ('twilight saints' centred in a window which, 'triple-arched', resembles the triptych of a church altar). This combination of physical warmth and spiritual coolness is epitomised in the view of Madeline kneeling where the pale light of the 'wintry moon' projects 'warm gules' onto her breast.

It is this perfect blend of physical ('rose-bloom') and spiritual ('silver') colouring that temporarily immobilises Porphyro. From his hiding place he regards the praying Madeline as if she were a saint, complete with halo, in a medieval painting. She is innocent, if deluded (in her trance she will yield herself to a real lover, not a mere vision). Piquancy is added to the portrait by her virginal state, and her admirer's conflicting emotions – delight at the idea of seducing 'so pure a thing' and veneration in the presence of a human creature 'so free from mortal taint' – almost render him senseless ('Porphyro grew faint'). He recollects himself, however, and prepares for the task of initiating this innocent 'dove' into the world of 'wolves and bears'.

The religious language in which Porphyro swathes his mistress ('Clasped like a missal where swart Paynims pray') and himself ('A famished pilgrim – saved by miracle': stanza XXXVIII) indicates that he dignifies his opportunism by regarding it as a sacrament rather than a rape, much as Othello attempts to justify his murder of Desdemona by calling it a 'sacrifice' (*Othello*, V, ii, 68); and in Keats's scheme he is probably right to do so. Madeline's fleshly substance is again stressed – her jewellery has been 'warmed' by contact with her body – but from her comparison to a 'mermaid' (a female hybrid lacking genitalia) she seems ignorant of her sexuality. Porphyro must break the 'charm' of her arrested development.

He must also teach her that love in the waking world is inseparable from sorrow, a conclusion that the 'perplexed' Madeline has already half-arrived at before sleep comes to 'enshade' her 'in forgetfulness divine' (in the words of 'To Sleep'). In her potential for instruction in the realities of life Madeline differs from Lamia, who is quite happy to 'unperplex bliss from its neighbour pain' ('Lamia', I, 192) and construct a spurious paradise on the basis of this bogus segregation. But it needs Porphyro to educate Madeline into the duality of full human life. Madeline's sleep, her relapsing into the 'lap of legends old', is a false 'haven', a retrogressive stupor of 'blinded' ignorance, an anaesthetised state where neither joy nor pain make any impression. Porphyro must arouse her from it and lead her onward, into the 'storm' of life where equal measures of 'sunshine' and 'rain' will be encountered. Madeline cannot go back through time and 'be a bud again'. She contains in herself an apparently ideal synthesis of human and heavenly, but this fusion will be of no consequence if it remains 'heart-stifled', buried within. Porphyro's assignment is to warm the inert Madeline with the flame of his love and his worldly experience, to coax the blossom from the bud.

6 KEATS'S CRITICS

6.1 NINETEENTH-CENTURY CRITICS

The first devastating blows to Keats's reputation were delivered in the late summer of 1818 by J. G. Lockhart in *Blackwood's Edinburgh Magazine* and J. W. Croker in the *Quarterly Review*. The latter placed Keats in the 'Cockney' school, 'which may be defined to consist of the most incongruous ideas in the most uncouth language'. The former recommended him to abandon his 'poetic mania' and return to his apothecary's shop. Although he put a brave face on these attacks, claiming that 'my own domestic criticism has given me pain without comparison beyond what Blackwood or the Quarterly could possibly inflict' (letter to J. A. Hessey, 8 October 1818), there is no doubt that Keats was hurt, financially at least, by such vitriolic condemnation. He may not have been, as Byron affirmed, 'snuffed out by an article', for such reviews were not the physiological cause of his tuberculosis. But they did put the public on its guard against Keats, thereby curtailing demand for his books and, because of his consequent inability to redeem his debts, frustrating his hopes of marriage to Fanny. Keats went to his death not knowing whether poetic recognition would ever be accorded him or whether his name was simply 'writ in water'.

His reputation was slowly established during the nineteenth century, often through a misreading of his qualities, and it was not until the twentieth century that a full appreciation was arrived at. Tennyson, for instance, popularised Keats through his own poetry which, with its clarity of image and less strenuous intellectual line, was more accessible than its model, of which it offered a kind of diluted version. In mid-century the Pre-Raphaelites seized upon the peripheral concerns of Keats – his antique trappings and chivalric *mise-en-scène* – and turned them into the central themes of their own poems and paintings, creating a nostalgic cult of the medieval for its own sake and not as a means through which to explore perennial issues of psychological substance.

Despite Keats's rising popularity in the nineteenth century, some prejudices about him were to endure until the twentieth. These were:

(i) That Keats had been killed by the critics. '"Who killed John Keats?" "I", says the Quarterly', according to Byron in 1821.

(ii) That his poems reveal an effeminate, weak personality. 'All he wanted was manly strength and fortitude', said William Hazlitt in 1824. Such a reading of Keats saw him as a fragile object unable to withstand the buffetings of normal life. It was not until 1880 that this verdict began to be reversed, with Matthew Arnold's discovery of 'flint and iron' and 'the elements of high character' in Keats.

(iii) That his poems display an absence of morality, owing to religious incertitude. 'His is a diseased state of feeling, arising from the want . . . of the regulating principle of religion', said Josiah Conder in 1820; and Coventry Patmore, reviewing Richard Milnes's *Life* of Keats in 1848, declared that 'a man without belief is like a man without backbone'.

(iv) That Keats died before realising his full promise – 'Just as he really promised something great' (Byron, *Don Juan*, XI, ix) – a myth finally dispelled, reversed even, by Francis Thompson's judgement in 1897 that Keats 'died in perfect time/In predecease of his just-sickening song' (The Cloud's Swan-song').

(v) That he was a poet of the senses, not the mind. '[Shelley] and Keats are both poets of sensation rather than reflection', wrote Arthur Hallam in 1831; and G. H. Lewes in 1848 said, 'He will always remain in our literature as a marvellous specimen of what mere sensuous imagery can create in poetry . . . He questioned nothing. He strove to penetrate no problems. He was content to feel and sing'. Keats's poetry, in other words, was devoid of intellectual energy. This view of Keats encouraged imitators, such as Oscar Wilde at the end of the century, to assume that Keats indulged in sensuous imagery for its own sake. The Aesthetic dedication to 'art for art's sake', based on the belief that art could and should be divorced from moral purpose, took its origin from an inadequate reading of Keats.

Another lasting prejudice denigrated Keats for his supposed low-class origins. This began with Lockhart's attack in *Blackwood's Edinburgh Magazine* on the 'rising brood of Cockneys', among whom Keats, as an apprentice apothecary, was castigated for his presumptuousness in aligning himself with Wordsworth, whose class connections were impeccable: 'The purest, the loftiest, and . . . the most classical of living English poets'. This snobbish disdain towards 'Johnny Keats' for daring to rise above his station among 'farm-servants' and 'footmen' extended to a general assumption that an apothecary's assistant must be devoid of the classical education necessary for writing poetry. 'John Keats . . . without Greek/ Contrived to talk about the gods of late', wrote Lord Byron, affecting astonishment, in *Don Juan*; and an unsigned review in the *London Magazine* of 1820 commented that Keats's 'knowledge of Greek and mythology seems to mystify him on every occasion'.

What was also difficult for his critics, even his publishers, to accept, was that a poet who was 'not a lord' (as Keats remarked sarcastically in one of his letters) should dare to write on the subjects of sex and politics. The conservative critics, annoyed by Keats's support of the liberal faction through his association with Leigh Hunt, wanted to put him back in his place: 'back to the shop, Mr John, back to "plasters, pills, and ointment boxes"', as Lockhart enjoined at the end of his review.

Other nineteenth-century critics chose more artistic grounds on which to attack Keats. Thomas Carlyle, for example, complained in 1871 about his cloying style ('Keats wanted a world of treacle!'), while Thomas de Quincey in 1845 took exception to Keats's violation of the English language: 'if there is one thing in this world that . . . should be holy in the eyes of a young poet, it is the *language* of his country', a language which, said de Quincey, Keats had 'trampled as with the hoofs of a buffalo'. For a complete and dispassionate appraisal of his worth as a poet Keats had to wait until the twentieth century.

6.2 TWENTIETH-CENTURY CRITICS

Keats has been battened on by modern critics, who find in him a wealth of material on which to feed their predilections; but these tend now to be the preferences of an individual rather than the prejudices of an era. F. R. Leavis, in *Revaluation* (1936), testifies to the modern consensus about Keats's poetic stature, while at the same time seeming to agree with the nineteenth-century opinion that he had been cut short before his prime, 'as if . . . the genius of a major poet were working in the material of a minor poetry'. Leavis's contemporary, T. S. Eliot, similarly finds that Keats's judgements on poetry as reflected in his letters reveal insight into 'a greater and more mature poetry than anything Keats ever wrote' (*The Use of Poetry and the Use of Criticism*, 1933).

Other critics focus on an unobtrusive aspect of Keats's poems and use it as a means of access to the poetry. Christopher Ricks, for example, in *Keats and Embarrassment* (1974) looks at instances of blushing in Keats's works, concluding that blushes in nature (the 'barred clouds', for example, which 'bloom the soft-dying day' in 'To Autumn') humanise the non-human, establishing an empathy be-

tween the poet and the 'other' world which he is a part of, yet
uniquely separate from: 'To be at one with the otherness of nature is
the arching complement to that other impulse, to be at one with the
otherness of other people'. The possibilities of discovering such
modes of ingress into the philosophy behind Keats's work are
seemingly endless.

A particularly fruitful line of enquiry has been that of critical
biography, which shows how the life and the works inform and enrich
each other. W. J. Bate (1963), Aileen Ward (1963) and Robert
Gittings (1968) are the three leading exponents of this approach. As
Gittings says at the end of *John Keats*, 'no part of Keats's life should
be neglected, and every incident, once recorded, may have immense
value in interpreting his poetry'. Bate's reading of 'The Fall of
Hyperion' benefits from his knowledge of the development of Keats's
ideas as gleaned from his letters. Thus the confrontation with Moneta
is that of 'the modern poet not merely with the accumulated
achievement of the past . . . but with the total accumulated experience of man'. Such criticism is often exhilarating to read, but is
unlikely to appeal to critics belonging to modern schools, such as
structuralism, which distrust biographical connections between the
author and the textual artifact.

Keats's poems are now being read from an infinitude of view-
points. One final example, touched on in the commentary on 'The
Eve of St Agnes', must suffice. Earl Wasserman (1953) relates the
poem to Keats's 'mansion of many apartments' letter and Wordsworth's 'Tintern Abbey', spiritualising Porphyro's sexual act as a step
towards a metaphysical state of being, and perhaps glossing over its
explicit physicality in the version censored by Keats's publisher
(whose reader, Woodhouse, complained that Porphyro 'acts all the
acts of a bona fide husband'). Jack Stillinger (1971), contrary to
Wasserman, sees Porphyro as an unprincipled seducer, and Madeline
as stupidly superstitious, paying the penalty for her arrested emotional development. Stillinger draws the moral that 'an individual
ought not to lose touch with the reality of this world'. Keats's poetry
is likely to provoke such widely differing interpretations as long as the
art of criticism endures.

REVISION QUESTIONS

1. To what extent is Keats a poet of sensuousness, and to what extent a poet of sense?

2. '*Endymion* contains in embryo many of the themes that are to be developed in the later poems'. Discuss.

3. How does Keats create atmosphere in *Isabella* and *The Eve of St Agnes*, and what relationship is there between atmosphere and theme?

4. What are the issues raised in any two of Keats's odes, and how does he attempt to resolve them?

5. Discuss the various female characters in Keats's narrative poems.

6. Analyse the argument and the imagery of any two of Keats's sonnets.

7. What is Keats's attitude towards nature on the evidence of his poems and/or his letters?

8. What is there in Keats's work that might entitle him to be considered a 'modern' poet?

9. Discuss Keats's manipulation of sound to echo the sense of his verse.

10. Discuss Keats's ideas about poetry and the role of the poet as they emerge from his poems and/or his letters.

11. In what ways is Keats a 'Romantic' poet?

12. Discuss the place of suffering in Keats's philosophy.

13. What do the urn and the nightingale symbolise in Keats's odes?

14. What are Keats's expectations of 'human passion', on the evidence of his writings?

15. Discuss the significance of imagination in Keats's poetry and/or his letters.

FURTHER READING

Texts

Barnard, John (ed.), *John Keats: The Complete Poems* (Penguin, 1973 – second edition 1977). This edition provides informative footnotes and biographical background to the composition of the poems, and a glossary of classical names.

Gittings, Robert (ed.), *Letters of John Keats: A Selection* (Oxford University Press, 1970 – reprinted 1985). All of Keats's most celebrated letters are collected in this edition.

Biographies

Bate, Walter Jackson, *John Keats* [1963] (Oxford University Press, 1967). An exhaustive study, with detailed analysis of the poems.

Gittings, Robert, *John Keats* [1968] (Penguin, 1979 – reprinted 1985). Particularly good on legal and financial details, and on the atmosphere of Keats's Regency England.

Criticism

Brooks, Cleanth, 'History without Footnotes: An Account of Keats's Urn', in *The Well Wrought Urn* [1947] (Methuen, 1968). An influential analysis of 'Ode on a Grecian Urn'.

Eliot, T. S., *The Use of Poetry and the Use of Criticism* (Faber, 1933). Contains a section on Keats's insight into the poetic craft.

Fraser, G. S. (ed.), *John Keats: The Odes: A Casebook* (Macmillan, 1971). A collection of seminal studies on the odes.

Mill, John Spencer (ed.), *Keats: The Narrative Poems: A Casebook* (Macmillan, 1983). Gathers together some vigorous and stimulating articles, many from contrasting points of view.

Leavis, F. R., 'Keats', in *Revaluation: Tradition and Development in English Poetry* (Chatto & Windus, 1936). Has influenced many subsequent critics.

Matthews, G. M. (ed.), *Keats: The Critical Heritage* (Routledge & Kegan Paul, 1971). Contains the most durable of the nineteenth-century criticism, as well as the vicious early reviews.

Ricks, Christopher, *Keats and Embarrassment* (Oxford University Press, 1974). Finds a way through to some of Keats's concerns by the unlikely entrance of the topic of blushing.

Ridley, M. R., *Keats's Craftsmanship: A Study in Poetic Development* (Clarendon Press, 1933). Examines Keats's painstaking drive to prosodic perfection.

Stillinger, Jack, *The Hoodwinking of Madeline and other Essays on Keats's Poems* (University of Illinois Press, 1971). A collection of thought-provoking articles; a healthy antidote to Wasserman.

Wasserman, Earl R., *The Finer Tone: Keats's Major Poems* (Johns Hopkins Press, 1953). Focuses on aspects of spiritual metamorphosis; persuasively argued, but criticised by Stillinger as too 'metaphysical' an approach.

Watts, Cedric, *A Preface to Keats* (Longman, 1985). A wide-ranging introductory study, with interesting illustrations, some more relevant than others.

Mastering English Literature
Richard Gill

Mastering English Literature will help readers both to enjoy English Literature and to be successful in 'O' levels, 'A' levels and other public exams. It is an introduction to the study of poetry, novels and drama which helps the reader in four ways - by providing ways of approaching literature, by giving examples and practice exercises, by offering hints on how to write about literature, and by the author's own evident enthusiasm for the subject. With extracts from more than 200 texts, this is an enjoyable account of how to get the maximum satisfaction out of reading, whether it be for formal examinations or simply for pleasure.

Work Out English Literature ('A' level)
S.H. Burton

This book familiarises 'A' level English Literature candidates with every kind of test which they are likely to encounter. Suggested answers are worked out step by step and accompanied by full author's commentary. The book helps students to clarify their aims and establish techniques and standards so that they can make appropriate responses to similar questions when the examination pressures are on. It opens up fresh ways of looking at the full range of set texts, authors and critical judgements and motivates students to know more of these matters.